OXFORD

Mastermaths 4

Paul Briten

Oxford University Press

Oxford University Press, Great Clarendon Street, Oxford OX2 6DP

Oxford New York
Auckland Bangkok Buenos Aires Cape Town Chennai
Dar es Salaam Delhi Hong Kong Istanbul Karachi Kolkata
Kuala Lumpur Madrid Melbourne Mexico City Mumbai Nairobi
São Paulo Singapore Taipei Tokyo Toronto

with an associated company in Berlin

Oxford is a trade mark of Oxford University Press

© Paul Briten 1997

First published 1984
Reprinted 1985, 1989, 1991, 1993, 1994 (twice)
New Edition 1997
Reprinted 1999, 2000, 2001, 2002

ISBN 0 19 834840 1

Typeset by Tradespools Ltd, Frome and Hardlines, Charlbury

Illustrated by CGS Studios, Cheltenham

Printed in Hong Kong

Contents

Contents

Assessment questions – key to levels:
black = level 3; blue = level 4; black in blue circle = level 5 and above

A 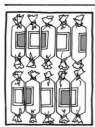 A box holds 10 crackers. How many boxes can be filled, and how many crackers left over with:

☆ 46 crackers? 4 boxes. 6 crackers left.

1	32 crackers?	6	28 crackers?
2	64 crackers?	7	99 crackers?
3	71 crackers?	8	12 crackers?
4	49 crackers?	9	40 crackers?
5	15 crackers?	10	90 crackers?

B  100 PINS / 100 DRAWING PINS

A packet holds 100 drawing pins. How many packets can be filled, and how many pins left over with:

☆ 286 pins? 2 packets. 86 pins left.

1	325 pins?	6	243 pins?
2	416 pins?	7	307 pins?
3	772 pins?	8	860 pins?
4	674 pins?	9	410 pins?
5	760 pins?	10	603 pins?

C 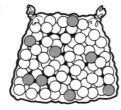 Counters are sold in bags of 1000. How many bags can be filled, and how many counters left over with:

☆ 6819 counters? 6 bags. 819 counters.

1	4273 counters?	6	2416 counters?
2	1685 counters?	7	1073 counters?
3	4270 counters?	8	2601 counters?
4	3608 counters?	9	4200 counters?
5	9437 counters?	10	7060 counters?

> is greater than

< is less than

D Write the sign $<$ or $>$ for $*$'s:

☆ 87 $*$ 78 $>$

1	64 $*$ 57	11	152 $*$ 251
2	83 $*$ 46	12	1634 $*$ 1436
3	23 $*$ 32	13	2424 $*$ 4242
4	44 $*$ 40	14	3363 $*$ 3336
5	66 $*$ 60	15	5910 $*$ 5019
6	162 $*$ 126	16	6198 $*$ 6189
7	624 $*$ 246	17	2663 $*$ 2636
8	224 $*$ 242	18	1110 $*$ 999
9	688 $*$ 668	19	1011 $*$ 1110
10	493 $*$ 394	20	1010 $*$ 1001

E Write the value of each **blue** number:

☆ 24**3**9   30

1	4**5**3	6	92**3**
2	**8**49	7	1**4**8
3	62**7**	8	**2**362
4	10**1**4	9	85**9**0
5	126**9**	10	1**7**00

F Write answers only:

☆ 60+80= $*$ 140

1	50+40= $*$	7	100+50= $*$
2	70+30= $*$	8	300+400= $*$
3	50+60= $*$	9	600+500= $*$
4	90+50= $*$	10	400+90= $*$
5	60+60= $*$	11	500+700= $*$
6	80+70= $*$	12	900+400= $*$

Crash landing

You need 28 counters.
Cover circles with the answers to the questions below.
Which 2 people will fall because their ropes have broken?

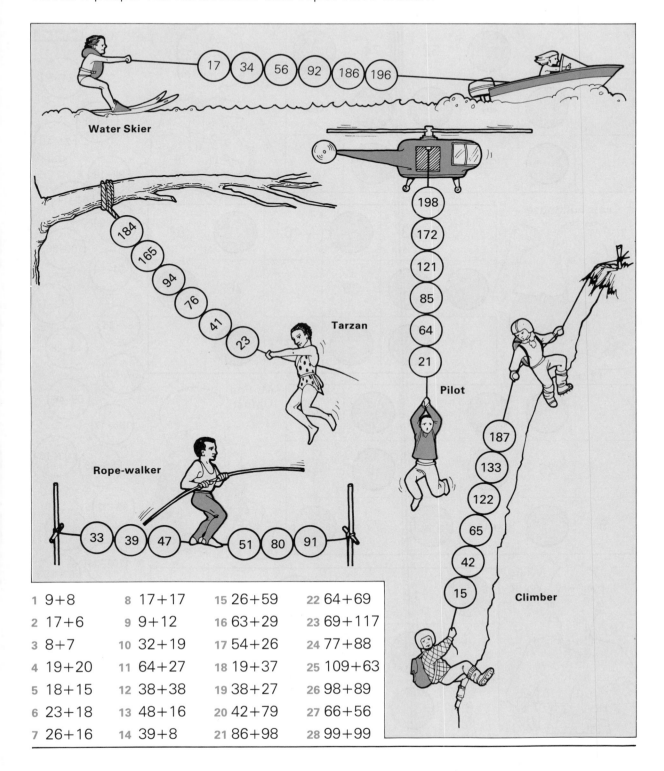

1 9+8	8 17+17	15 26+59	22 64+69
2 17+6	9 9+12	16 63+29	23 69+117
3 8+7	10 32+19	17 54+26	24 77+88
4 19+20	11 64+27	18 19+37	25 109+63
5 18+15	12 38+38	19 38+27	26 98+89
6 23+18	13 48+16	20 42+79	27 66+56
7 26+16	14 39+8	21 86+98	28 99+99

You need 25 counters.
Cover the board numbers that give the answers to these questions.
Who wins the Bingo game?

Mrs Winalot

	17	●	52	74	●
6	●	34	●	●	83
	●	35	57	●	

Ivor Fullhouse

	23	●	46	●	81
●	●	39		76	●
14	●	●	67	●	

Mr Phil Upfast

7	●	●		●	84
	25	●	58	●	
9	●	40	●	77	●

Willie Winit

●	18	29	●	64	80
	●	●	49	●	
8	●		●	●	90

24–7
16–9
21–15
32–18
51–17
80–22
100–26
54–19
63–17
82–25
46–28
87–58
69–46
100–17
93–16
88–39
96–32
84–17
101–11
93–85
71–46
92–53
100–16
71–19
100–60

Place value

Sometimes you must count accurately.

Sometimes you do not need an exact number. You can round off:

John has 82 marbles.

82 is nearer to 80 than to 90.
He says he has about 80 marbles.

Nirma has 168 books. She says she has about 170 books.

They have rounded off the numbers to the nearest 10.

You can round off to the nearest 100.
563 people went to the Village Fair.

563 is nearer to 600 than to 500.
The mayor said that about 600 people went to the Fair.

B **Round off** these numbers **to the nearest 100**:

☆ 1260   1300

1	276	6	4274
2	184	7	3614
3	723	8	4249
4	949	9	6390
5	380	10	2807

C **Round off** these prices **to the nearest £100**:

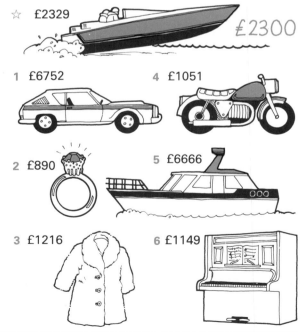

☆ £2329   £2300

1 £6752   4 £1051

2 £890   5 £6666

3 £1216   6 £1149

A **Round off** these numbers **to the nearest 10**:

☆ 169   170

1	92	*90*	11	389 *390*
2	57	*60*	12	297 *300*
3	63	*60*	13	418 *420*
4	48	*50*	14	991 *990*
5	29	*30*	15	1253 *1250*
6	56	*60*	16	2468 *2470*
7	116	*120*	17	3121 *3120*
8	191	*200*	18	4064 *4060*
9	237	*240*	19	1207 *1210*
10	258	*260*	20	2008 *2010*

Trevor has 165 stamps and he
wants to round this number
to the nearest 10.

165

| 120 | 130 | 140 | 150 | 160 | 170 | 180 |

165 comes halfway between 160 and 170.
Halfway numbers are rounded upwards.
Trevor says he has about 170 stamps.

On Saturday 3250 people
visited Prestwick Museum.

Lord Prestwick wants to
round this number to the nearest 100.

3250

| 3000 | 3100 | 3200 | 3300 | 3400 | 3500 | 3600 | 3700 |

3250 is halfway between 3200 and 3300.
Halfway numbers are rounded upwards.
Lord Prestwick says that about 3300
people visited the museum.

A The collections below were made by
the children in Trevor's class. **Round
off to the nearest 10** the number in
each collection:

☆ Jane has 165
coins

about 170 coins

1 Jo has 195
snails

2 Alex has 65
shells

3 Jean has 115
books

4 Jackie has 335
stamps

5 Bill has 85 rocks

6 Sandra has 205
postcards

B **Round off to the nearest 100** the
number of items in each of these
museum collections:

☆

2350 rocks

about 2400 rocks

1

250 fossils

2

1650 butterflies

3

8750 stamps

4

550 pictures

5

950 pressed
flowers

6

1050 pots

Place value

You can **round off to the nearest 1000**. The height of Mount McKinley in Alaska is 6189 m.

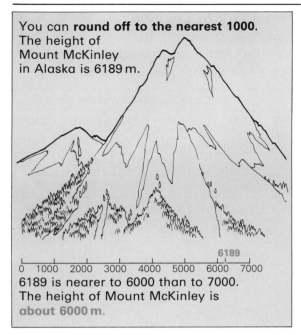

6189 is nearer to 6000 than to 7000. The height of Mount McKinley is about 6000 m.

8500 people watched Kickem Rovers play football.

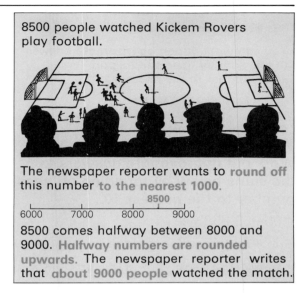

The newspaper reporter wants to round off this number to the nearest 1000.

8500 comes halfway between 8000 and 9000. Halfway numbers are rounded upwards. The newspaper reporter writes that about 9000 people watched the match.

A Copy and complete this table:

	town	population	population to the nearest 1000
☆	Aberdour	1587	2000
1	Baldock	6472	
2	Ellesmere	2719	
3	Ilfracombe	9462	
4	Long Melford	2891	
5	Winkfield	8764	
6	Ninfield	1111	
7	Pickering	4870	
8	Selsey	6506	
9	Llangefni	4169	

B Write these numbers **to the nearest 1000**:

☆ 3869   4000

1 6815   5 4560
2 4920   6 6049
3 6051   7 9499
4 7655   8 1234

C **Round off** these attendance numbers to the nearest 1000.

	team	attendance	
☆	Masham United	4500	5000
1	Clumsy Trippers	6500	
2	Windy Rovers	2650	
3	Muddle Town	9500	
4	Velos City	3850	
5	Forest Rangers	500	

D **Round off to the nearest £1000** the costs of these cars:

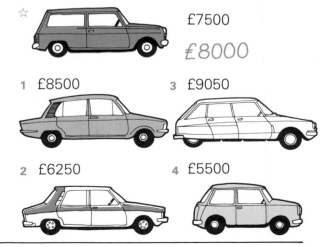

☆ £7500   £8000

1 £8500   3 £9050

2 £6250   4 £5500

69+42+53= ✳

You can work out an **approximate** answer to this sum by first rounding off each number **to the nearest 10**:

70+40 +50 = ✳

Approximate answer 160

A Work out **approximate** answers to the sums below by rounding off each number **to the nearest 10**.

70
80
+60
210

☆ 65+82+58= ✳

1 37+52+45= ✳

2 63+27+31= ✳ 6 91+70+56= ✳

3 26+53+52= ✳ 7 20+17+14= ✳

4 71+54+89= ✳ 8 54+86+85= ✳

5 25+32+66= ✳ 9 62+99+15= ✳

B

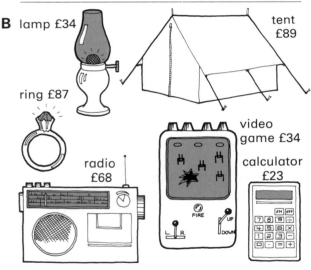

lamp £34

tent £89

ring £87

radio £68

video game £34

calculator £23

Round the costs above **to the nearest £10** and work out the **approximate** cost of:

☆ a lamp, a radio and a ring £190

1 a calculator and a video game

2 a radio and a tent

3 a calculator, a radio and a ring

4 a tent, a lamp and a radio

5 a video game, a ring and a calculator

C Round off **to the nearest 100** each figure in the table below.
Work out the **approximate** total sale for each item:

Crumb's bakery sales				
item	Jan	Feb	Mar	total
☆ doughnuts	2160	2380	1945	6500
1 loaves	2942	3264	2279	
2 scones	754	689	521	
3 rolls	1279	1480	1111	
4 buns	2620	1469	3482	
5 pies	996	1231	1012	
6 tarts	1163	1497	2019	

D Mr Phil Up owns 2 petrol stations. The table below shows his sales. Round each figure **to the nearest 1000**. Write down the **approximate** difference between each day's sales at the 2 stations:

day	Station Alpha (litres)	Station Omega (litres)	approximate difference (litres)
☆ Sunday	8670	4240	5000l
1 Monday	7962	3500	
2 Tuesday	7496	3850	
3 Wed.	8629	2347	
4 Thursday	9302	4817	
5 Friday	9229	2469	
6 Saturday	7770	3203	

Place value

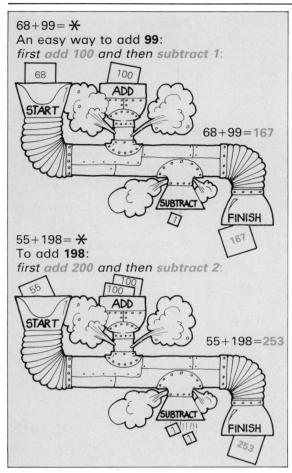

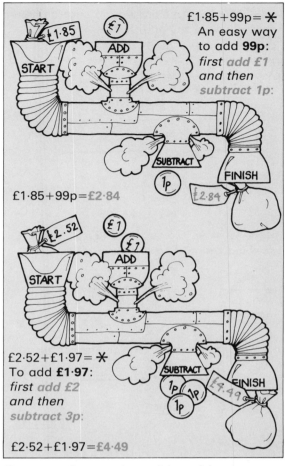

A Copy and complete this table:

	To add	first add	then subtract
☆	297	300	3
1	98		
2	199		
3	197		
4	397		
5	298		

C Copy and complete this table:

	To add	first add	then subtract
☆	£1·99	£2	1p
1	98p		
2	£1·98		
3	£2·99		
4	97p		
5	£2·96		

B Write answers only:

☆ 162+98   260

1 82+199= ✱
2 35+98= ✱
3 124+197= ✱
4 263+99= ✱
5 142+297= ✱
6 326+198= ✱
7 425+96= ✱
8 621+298= ✱

D Write answers only:

☆ £1·63+£1·98   £3·61

1 £1·24+98p= ✱
2 £1·63+99p= ✱
3 £2·55+£1·99= ✱
4 £2·30+£1·97= ✱
5 £6·23+£2·98= ✱
6 £3·65+£0·97= ✱
7 £6·66+£1·96= ✱
8 £3·82+£1·97= ✱

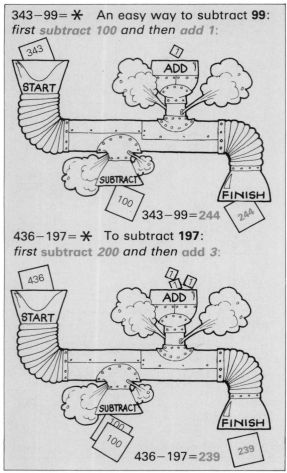

343−99= ✱   An easy way to subtract **99**:
first subtract 100 and then add 1:

343−99=**244**

436−197= ✱   To subtract **197**:
first subtract 200 and then add 3:

436−197=**239**

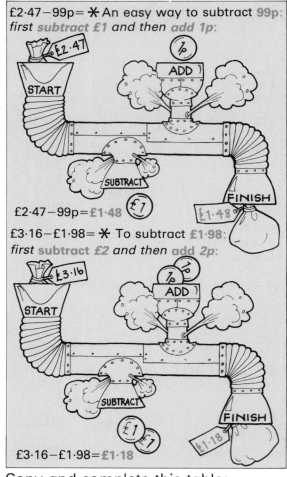

£2·47−99p= ✱ An easy way to subtract **99p**:
first subtract £1 and then add 1p:

£2·47−99p=**£1·48**

£3·16−£1·98= ✱ To subtract **£1·98**:
first subtract £2 and then add 2p:

£3·16−£1·98=**£1·18**

A Copy and complete this table:

	To subtract	first subtract	then add
☆	297	300	3
1	98		
2	97		
3	198		
4	199		
5	298		

B Write answers only:

☆ 456−198= ✱ 258

1 377−99= ✱   5 377−98= ✱
2 248−97= ✱   6 249−196= ✱
3 356−198= ✱   7 865−298= ✱
4 645−299= ✱   8 964−196= ✱

C Copy and complete this table:

	To subtract	first subtract	then add
☆	£2·98	£3	2p
1	£0·98		
2	97p		
3	£1·99		
4	£2·97		
5	£1·96		

D Write answers only:

☆ £3·45−£1·98= ✱ £1·47

1 £4·24−£1·97= ✱   5 £3·55−£2·99= ✱
2 £5·69−£0·99= ✱   6 £2·79−£1·98= ✱
3 £3·86−98p= ✱   7 £6·74−£2·97= ✱
4 £4·63−£1·98= ✱   8 £5·50−£1·96= ✱

A Write the value of each **blue** number:

1 2**6**8   *Tens*
2 **3**95   *Hundreds*
3 16**4**4   *Tens*
4 95**8**   *Units*
5 273**7**   *Units*
6 4**9**55   *Hundreds*
7 2**6**3   *Tens*
8 4**2**00   *Hundreds*
9 **5**396   *Thousands*
10 **7**10   *Hundreds*

B **Round off** these numbers **to the nearest 10**:

1 67   *70*
2 142   *140*
3 96   *100*
4 85   *90*
5 744   *740*
6 627   *630*
7 898   *900*
8 1275   *1280*
9 2345   *2350*
10 1009   *1010*

C **Round off** these prices **to the nearest £100**:

1 £486   *£500*
2 £927   *£900*
3 £650   *£700*
4 £1283   *£1300*
5 £2107   *£2100*
6 £3525   *£3500*
7 £2650   *£2700*
8 £4171   *£4200*
9 £1273   *£1300*
10 £6250   *£6300*

D **Round off** these distances **to the nearest 1000 km**:

1 4281 km
2 1765 km
3 3210 km
4 5320 km
5 4500 km
6 7251 km
7 3149 km
8 2500 km
9 8500 km
10 9271 km

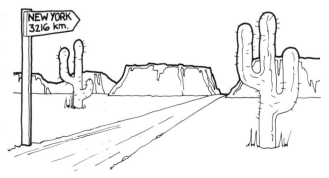

E Work out **approximate** answers to the sums below by rounding off each number **to the nearest 10**:

1 $46+52+61=$ *
2 $22+71+85=$ *
3 $47+40+33=$ *
4 $96+41+37=$ *
5 $64+25+25=$ *
6 $82+76+103=$ *
7 $48+9+17=$ *
8 $60+19+7=$ *
9 $72+48+201=$ *
10 $65+111+222=$ *

F Work out **approximate** answers to the sums below by rounding off each number **to the nearest 100**:

1 $325+694+276=$ *
2 $466+644+850=$ *
3 $772+184+684=$ *
4 $261+162+621=$ *
5 $555+444+610=$ *
6 $424+244+442=$ *
7 $650+109+257=$ *
8 $254+649+780=$ *
9 $362+195+666=$ *
10 $247+350+449=$ *

G Write answers only:

1 $67+99=$ *
2 $46+98=$ *
3 $185+99=$ *
4 $26+199=$ *
5 $132+198=$ *
6 $257+96=$ *
7 $124+298=$ *
8 $120+399=$ *
9 $367+298=$ *
10 $421+397=$ *

H Write answers only:

1 $127-99=$ *
2 $423-98=$ *
3 $241-199=$ *
4 $365-198=$ *
5 $342-96=$ *
6 $278-197=$ *
7 $821-298=$ *
8 $858-296=$ *
9 $568-297=$ *
10 $729-398=$ *

A Copy and complete this price chain:

	price	cost to nearest £1	cost to nearest £10	cost to nearest £100
	£864.86	£865		

Write a set of prices for the 6 empty boxes below so that:
a) the bicycle costs £21·50 more than the video
b) the video costs £63·80 more than the bicycle.

	price	cost to nearest £1	cost to nearest £10	cost to nearest £100
				£300
				£300

B How much money would a shopkeeper gain or lose if the prices of these items are rounded to the nearest £10?

£47.63 £65.99 £153.62 £327.90 £275.50

Choose a page from a shopping catalogue on which all of the items cost more than £10.

Work out how much money would be gained or lost if all of the prices are rounded to the nearest £10 and 1 of each item is sold.

Find a car sales advert in a newspaper. If the price of each car in the advert is rounded to the nearest £1000, find out how much money will be gained or lost when all of the cars are sold.

C Write clues for this crossword.

All the questions should ask for numbers to be rounded to the nearest 10, 100 or 1000.

The clues you need are:

across: 1, 3, 4, 5, 6, 9, 10, 11, 12, 13 and 14.

down: 1, 2, 3, 5, 7, 8, 10, 11 and 12.

Crossword grid:

¹8	²6	0		³9	0
⁴7	0		⁵7	0	
⁶9	0	⁷6	0		⁸4
0		⁹7	0	¹⁰9	0
	¹¹4	0		¹²8	0
¹³8	0		¹⁴5	0	0

Answer any questions you can. Leave those you cannot do.

Round off these journey distances to the nearest 10 km:

1 13 km

2 97 km

3 75 km

4 786 km

5 632 km

6 445 km

7 1276 km

8 8495 km

Round off these prices to the nearest £100

9 £6271

10 £5581

11 £10 219

12 £16 450

£1.98   99p   £3.02   £6.97

What is the total cost of:

13 a book and a tape?

14 a pen and a cake?

15 a book and a pen?

16 a tape, a cake and a book?

Fish sold at Take Your Plaice Fish Shop

	Jan	Feb	Mar
Cod	684	799	587
Haddock	476	624	455
Plaice	291	310	204
Monkfish	333	312	292
Salmon	140	126	95

To the nearest 100, at Take Your Plaice Fish Shop, what is the total sale of:

17 haddock and cod in January?

18 plaice and monk fish in March?

19 salmon in January, February and March?

20 salmon, plaice and cod in February?

21 cod and monk fish in February and March?

Football supporters

match	attendance
Arsenal v Spurs	29 264
Barcelona v Newcastle	35 496
Coventry v Aston Villa	17 901
Manchester Utd. v Liverpool	45 755
Rangers v Celtic	30 209
West Ham v Chelsea	32 500

To the nearest 1000, how many people watched the football match between:

22 Arsenal and Spurs?

23 Coventry and Aston Villa?

24 Manchester United and Liverpool?

25 Rangers and Celtic?

26 Barcelona and Newcastle?

27 West Ham and Chelsea?

Round these numbers to the nearest 10 000:

28 65 934

29 86 666

30 105 621

31 345 678

A Write the name of each **solid shape** and name the **shaded face**:

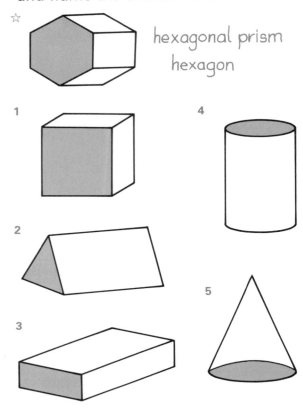

☆ hexagonal prism
hexagon

1

2

3

4

5

B Write the names of the shapes formed by these frameworks:

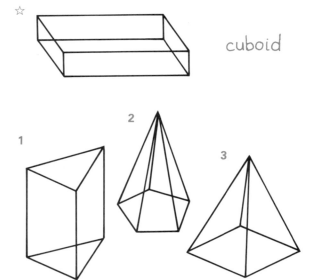

☆ cuboid

1

2

3

This solid shape is called a sphere.

C Where would you find these **spheres**?

☆ on a snooker table

1

2

3

4

D Try to explain why:

☆ marbles are spheres and not cones
so that they will roll in straight lines

1 footballs are spheres and not cubes

2 baked bean tins are cylinders and not spheres

3 building blocks are cubes and not spheres

4 ten pin bowls are spheres and not cylinders

Shape

This builder is fitting a pane of frosted glass. The smooth side of the glass must face outwards. He can fit the glass in two different ways.

A In how many ways will a pane of frosted glass fit into these window frames with the smooth side outwards?

☆

3

1

4

2

5

3

6

B 1 Trace the first shape below marking the centre dot.

2 Rotate your tracing through 360° on top of its shape, keeping the centre dots in line.

3 In how many different positions will the tracing fit exactly onto the shape?

4 Do the same for each of the other shapes.

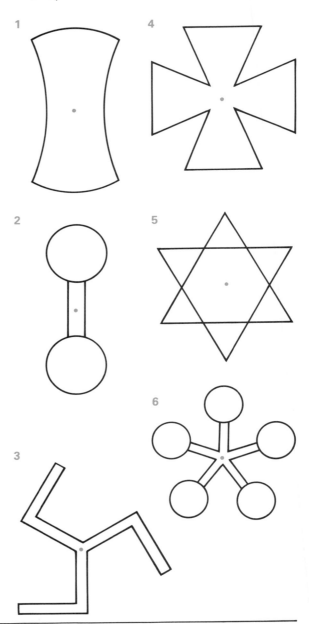

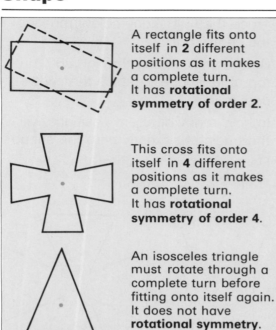

A rectangle fits onto itself in **2** different positions as it makes a complete turn. It has **rotational symmetry of order 2.**

This cross fits onto itself in **4** different positions as it makes a complete turn. It has **rotational symmetry of order 4.**

An isosceles triangle must rotate through a complete turn before fitting onto itself again. It does not have **rotational symmetry.**

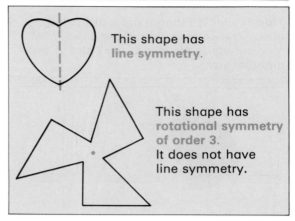

This shape has line symmetry.

This shape has rotational symmetry of order 3. It does not have line symmetry.

A Take tracings if you need to. Work out the **order of rotational symmetry** for each shape below:

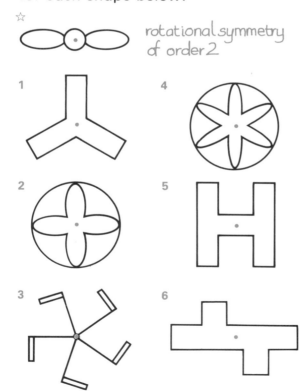

☆ rotational symmetry of order 2

B Answer these questions for each shape:
Does it have **line symmetry**?
What is the order of **rotational symmetry**?

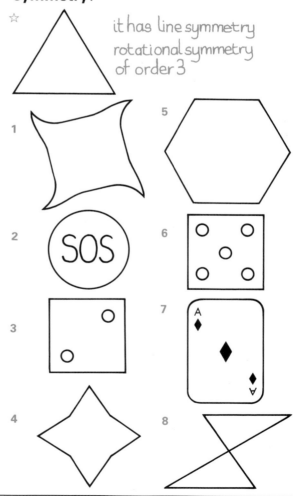

☆ it has line symmetry rotational symmetry of order 3

Shape

A Answer these questions:

☆ What is the order of rotational symmetry of this shape? 2

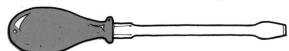

In how many different positions can this screwdriver be placed on the screw? 2

1 What is the order of rotational symmetry of this shape?

In how many different positions can the screwdriver be placed on the screw?

2 What is the order of rotational symmetry of this shape?

In how many different positions can the wheel be fitted onto the car?

3 What is the order of rotational symmetry of this shape?

In how many different positions can the key be fitted into the clock?

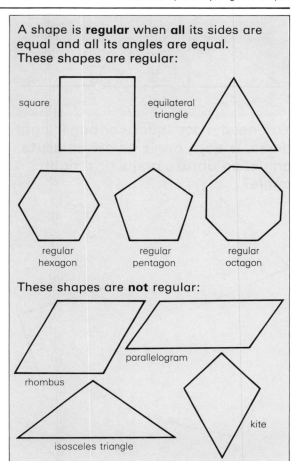

A shape is **regular** when **all** its sides are equal and all its angles are equal. These shapes are regular:

square
equilateral triangle
regular hexagon
regular pentagon
regular octagon

These shapes are **not** regular:

rhombus
parallelogram
isosceles triangle
kite

B Copy and complete this table:

	shape	number of lines of symmetry	order of rotational symmetry
☆	square	4	4
1	equilateral triangle		
2	regular hexagon		
3	regular pentagon		
4	regular octagon		
5	rhombus		
6	parallelogram		
7	kite		
8	isosceles triangle		

C What does the table tell you about all regular shapes?

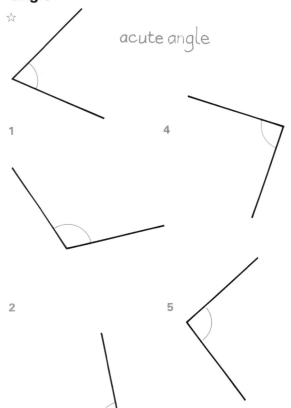

acute angle   right angle   obtuse angle

A You need a set square or paper right angle. Is each angle below an **acute angle**, an **obtuse angle** or a **right angle**?

☆ acute angle

1

4

2

5

3

6

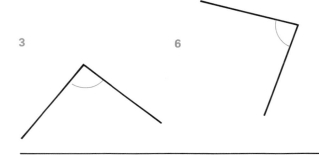

B How many **degrees** is:

☆ 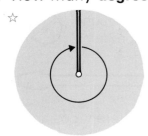 a complete turn?

360°

1 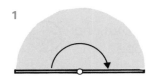 half a turn?

2 a quarter turn or 1 right angle?

3  ½ a right angle?

C Are these angles **acute angles** or **obtuse angles**?

☆ 86°   acute

1	38°	6	83°	11 164°
2	127°	7	49°	12 100°
3	154°	8	92°	13 91°
4	98°	9	61°	14 89°
5	62°	10	88°	15 99°

D Write these angles in **degrees**:

☆ $2\frac{1}{2}$ right angles   90°+90°+45°=225°

1 2 right angles

2 3 right angles

3 4 right angles

4 $1\frac{1}{2}$ right angles

5 $3\frac{1}{2}$ right angles

Angles

You can use a **protractor** for measuring angles.

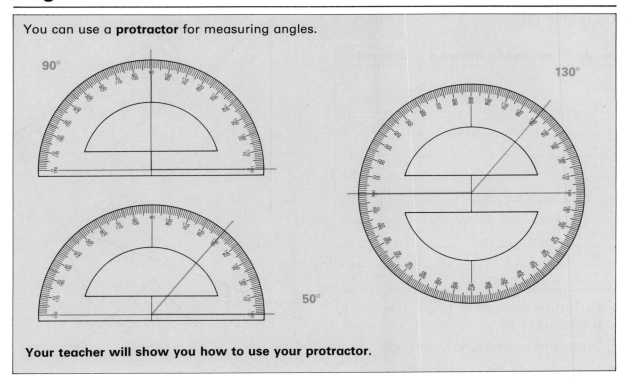

Your teacher will show you how to use your protractor.

A Use your **protractor** to measure
these angles:

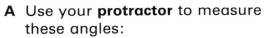

☆ 70°

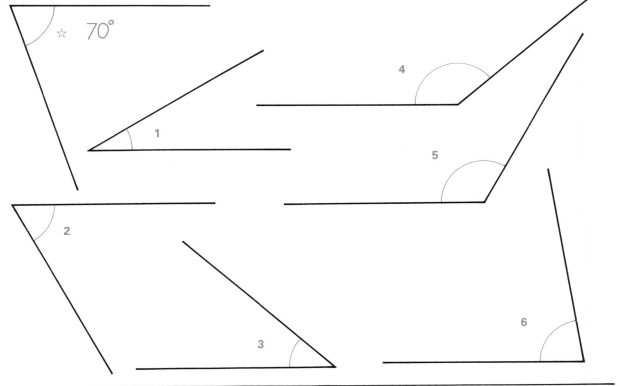

A Copy this table:

angle	estimate	measure	difference
1			
2			
3			
4			
5			
6			
7			
8			
9			

B 1 **Estimate** the size of angle 1 below to the nearest 10°.

2 Write the estimate in your table.

3 Use a protractor to **measure** angle 1.

4 Write your measure in the table.

5 Work out the **difference** between your estimate and the measure.

6 Write the difference in the table.

7 Do the same for the other angles.

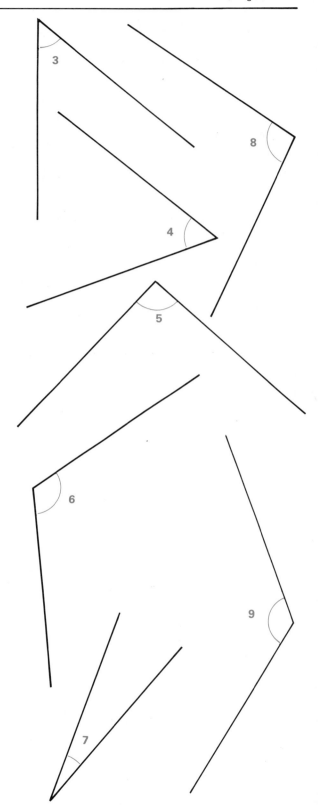

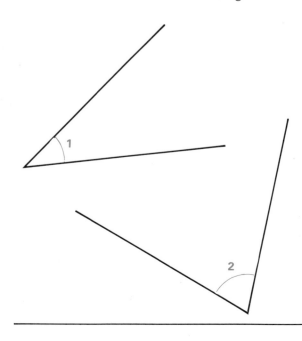

Angles

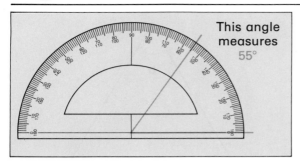

This angle measures 55°

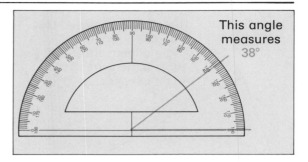

This angle measures 38°

A You need a **protractor**.
Measure these angles:

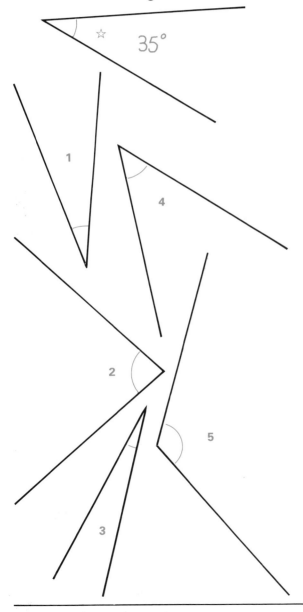

☆ 35°

1

4

2

5

3

B You need a **protractor**.
Measure these angles as accurately as you can:

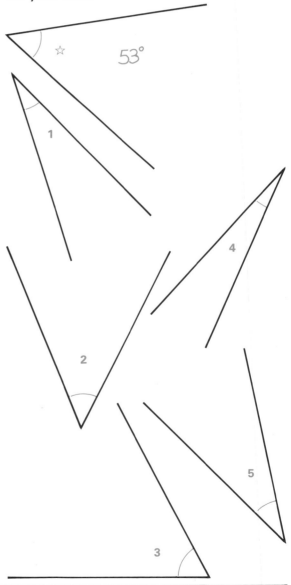

☆ 53°

1

4

2

5

3

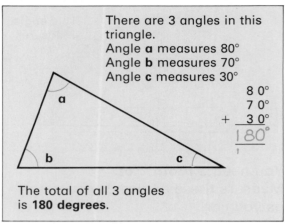

There are 3 angles in this triangle.
Angle **a** measures 80°
Angle **b** measures 70°
Angle **c** measures 30°

8 0°
7 0°
+ 3 0°
180°

The total of all 3 angles is **180 degrees**.

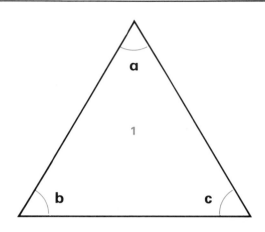

A Copy this table:

triangle	angle			total of all 3 angles
	a	**b**	**c**	
☆	40°	50°	90°	180°
1				
2				
3				
4				

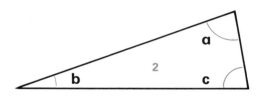

B 1 Measure the 3 angles in each triangle.

2 Write the measures in your table.

3 Work out the total of all 3 angles in each triangle.

4 Write the totals in your table.

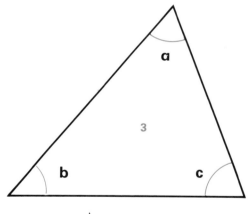

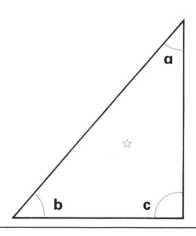

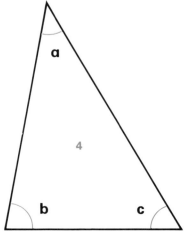

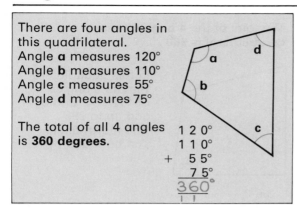

There are four angles in
this quadrilateral.
Angle **a** measures 120°
Angle **b** measures 110°
Angle **c** measures 55°
Angle **d** measures 75°

The total of all 4 angles
is **360 degrees**.

$$\begin{aligned} 1\,2\,0° \\ 1\,1\,0° \\ +\quad 5\,5° \\ \underline{7\,5°} \\ 360° \end{aligned}$$

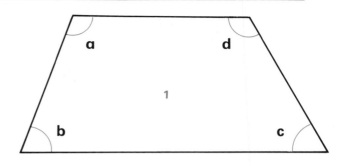

A Copy this table:

quadrilateral	angles				total of all 4 angles
	a	b	c	d	
☆	80°	85°	130°	65°	360°
1					
2					
3					
4					

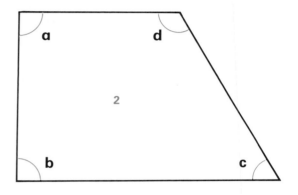

B 1 Measure the 4 angles in each
quadrilateral.

2 Write the measures in your table.

3 Work out the total of all 4 angles in
each quadrilateral.

4 Write the totals in your table.

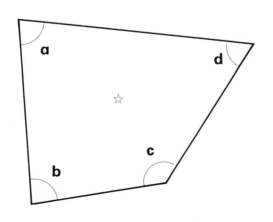

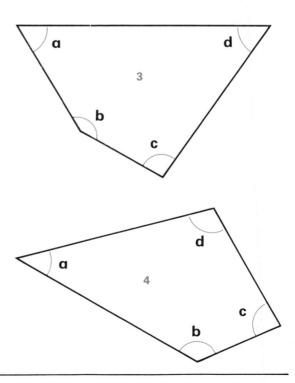

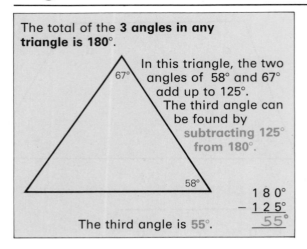

The total of the **3 angles in any triangle is 180°**.

In this triangle, the two angles of 58° and 67° add up to 125°.
The third angle can be found by **subtracting 125° from 180°**.

```
  1 8 0°
−  1 2 5°
    5 5°
```

The third angle is **55°**.

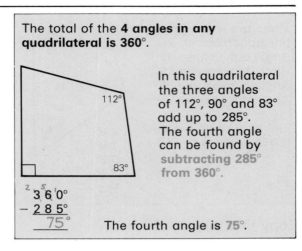

The total of the **4 angles in any quadrilateral is 360°**.

In this quadrilateral the three angles of 112°, 90° and 83° add up to 285°.
The fourth angle can be found by **subtracting 285° from 360°**.

```
  ²3⁵6 0°
−  2 8 5°
     7 5°
```

The fourth angle is **75°**.

A Do not use a protractor. Work out the size of the angle marked ✳ in each triangle:

B Do not use a protractor. Work out the size of the angle marked ✳ in each quadrilateral:

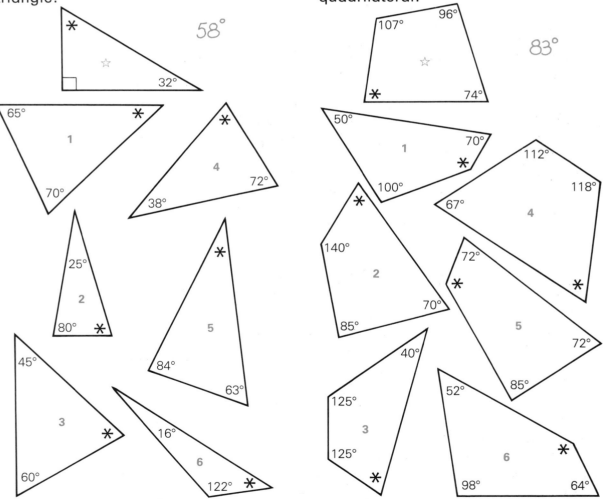

Angles

A These cakes have been cut into 6 pieces. Measure the angle at the centre of the cake for each piece:

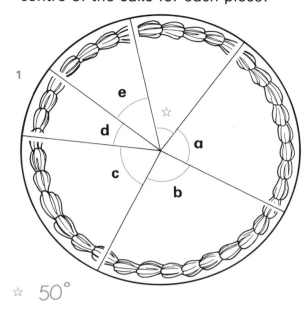

1

☆ 50°

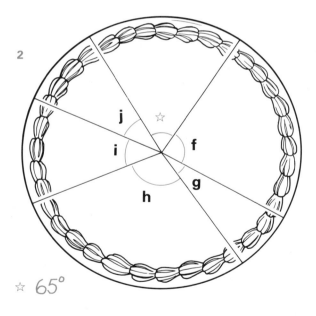

2

☆ 65°

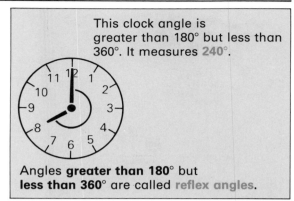

This clock angle is greater than 180° but less than 360°. It measures **240°**.

Angles **greater than 180°** but **less than 360°** are called reflex angles.

B Use a circular protractor to measure these **reflex angles**:

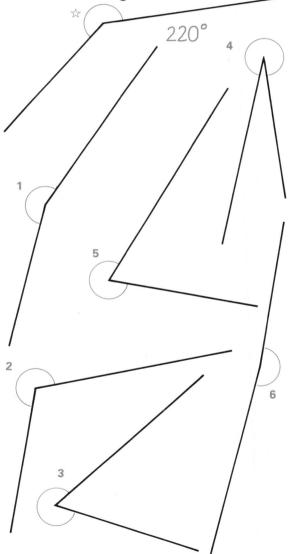

☆ 220°

beach

lighthouse

cliffs

wreck

weathership

reef

harbour

coastguard

N

rocks

ship

submarine

buoy

pleasure boat

cruiser

yacht

To fix his position, the captain of the ship takes bearings.

A bearing is the angle measured clockwise, between North and the object.
A bearing always has 3 figures.

The bearing of the lighthouse from the ship is: 030°.
The bearing of the yacht from the ship is 210°.

A You need a circular protractor. Work out the **bearing** from the ship, of:

☆ the rocks   255°

1 the wreck	7 the beach
2 the reef	8 the submarine
3 the harbour	9 the weathership
4 the buoy	10 the coastguard
5 the cliffs	11 the pleasure boat
6 the cruiser	12 the lighthouse

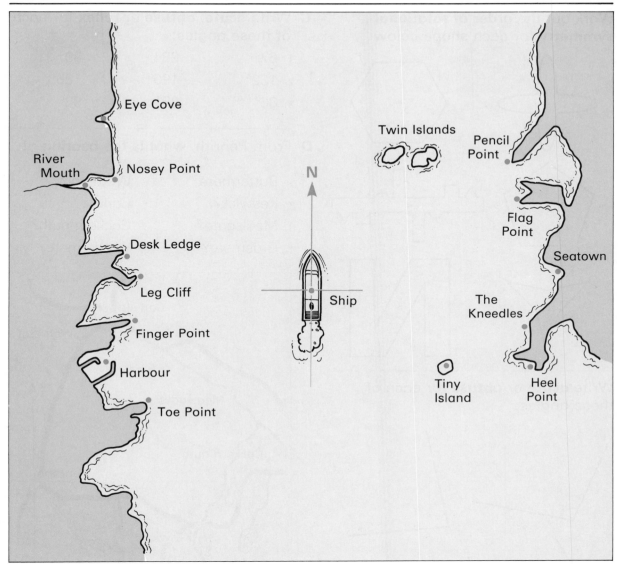

A If this ship sails East, it must sail on a **bearing** of **090°**. On what **bearing** must the ship sail to go:

☆ South? *180°*

1 West?

2 North East?

3 South West?

4 South East?

5 North West?

6 to Finger Point?

7 to the harbour?

8 to Desk Ledge?

9 to Flag Point?

10 to Seatown?

11 to Tiny Island?

12 to Nosey Point?

B Choose the correct **course** for the ship to sail:

☆ between Twin Islands
125° 020° 035° 045° *035°*

1 to Toe Point 045° 055° 155° 235°

2 to Heel Point 020° 110° 160° 120°

3 to the Kneedles 100° 170° 010° 090°

4 to Leg Cliff 005° 275° 185° 265°

5 to River Mouth 025° 165° 285° 295°

6 to Eye Cove 040° 310° 325° 120°

7 to Pencil Point 045° 125° 055° 060°

A Work out the **order of rotational symmetry** for each shape below:

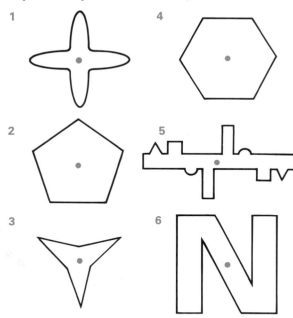

B Write **acute** or **obtuse** for each of these angles:

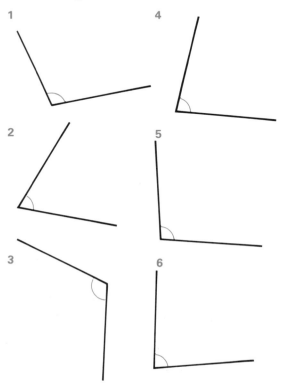

C Write **acute**, **obtuse** or **reflex** for each of these angles:

1 67°	4 284°	7 89°
2 132°	5 190°	8 185°
3 86°	6 28°	9 93°

D From Penrith, what is the **bearing** of:

1 Buttermere?   5 Wetheral?

2 Keswick?   6 Carlisle?

3 Mealsgate?   7 Cockermouth?

4 Grasmere?   8 Windermere?

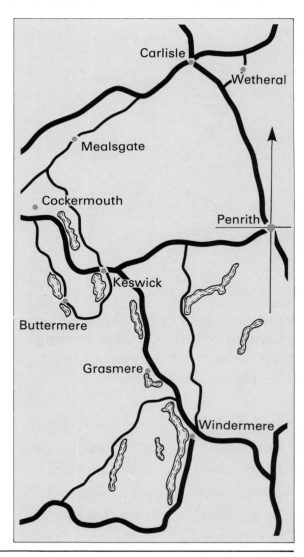

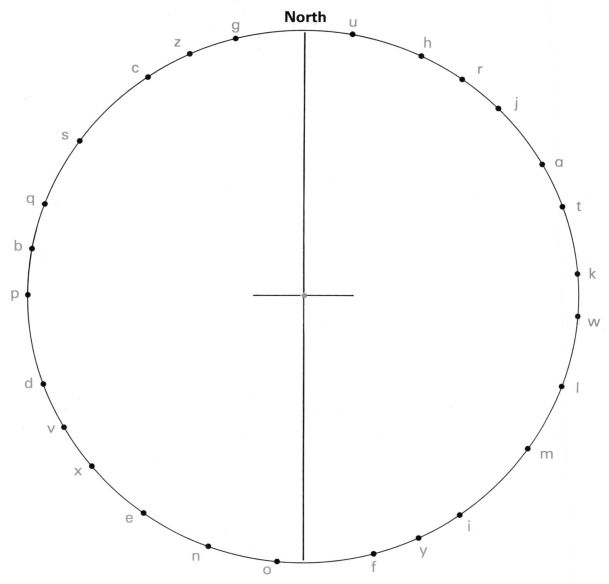

A Take the **bearings** written below from the **blue** dot. Write the letters on each bearing to find a message.

☆ for 095° write   w

Word 1: 095° 025° 060° 070°

Word 2: 145° 305°

Word 3: 070° 025° 215°

Word 4: 070° 145° 070° 110° 215°

Word 5: 185° 165°

Word 6: 155° 185° 010° 035°

Word 7: 165° 060° 240° 185° 010° 035° 145° 070° 215°

Word 8: 270° 145° 215° 325° 215°

Word 9: 185° 165°

Word 10: 125° 010° 305° 145° 325°

B Answer the message by writing bearings for letters.
Example: instead of **i** write **145°**.

A Design a logo with rotational symmetry of order 4 for a company that sells flowers.

Design a logo with rotational symmetry of order 3 for a company that sells art equipment.

B Draw a circle with a radius of approximately 4 cm. Mark a dot at the centre of the circle.

Mark 12 equally spaced points on the circumference by carefully measuring 30° angles at the centre.

Join each point on the circumference to every other point.

On your drawing find an example of:

a) an equilateral triangle.   b) a regular hexagon.   c) a regular dodecahedron. (12 sided shape)   d) a rectangle.

Outline each shape with a coloured pen.

What is the order of rotational symmetry for each of these shapes?

C You need: a playing board, 16 cards of the same size on which are drawn angles of 5° 10° 15° 20° 25° 30° 35° 40° 45° 50° 55° 60° 70° 75° 85° and 90°, two sets of 6 coloured counters, a partner.

60°	35°	10°	55°
85°	45°	5°	75°
30°	40°	20°	15°
25°	50°	70°	90°

Shuffle the cards and place them face down on the table.

The first player turns over the top card and tries to match the angle with one of the angles written on the playing board.

The second player checks the estimate using a protractor.

If the estimate was correct the first player covers the angle on the playing board with a counter and removes the angle card from the game. If the estimate was wrong, no counter is placed on the playing board and the angle card is returned to the bottom of the pack.

Players take turns in this way until one player forms an unbroken straight line of 3 counters or has 6 counters on the playing board. This player is the winner.

Answer any questions you can. Leave those you cannot do.

What is the order of rotational symmetry for each of these shapes?

1

2

3

4

5

What is the order of rotational symmetry of

6 an equilateral triangle?

7 a square?

8 a parallelogram?

9 a rhombus?

Use a protractor to measure these angles. Say for each angle whether it is acute, obtuse or reflex:

10

11

12

13

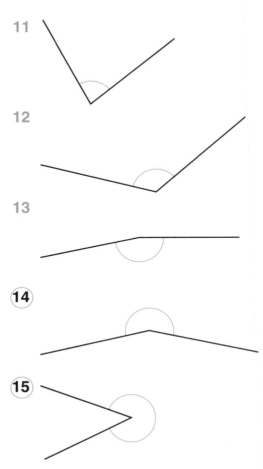

14

15

What is the size of each of these missing angles?

16

17

18

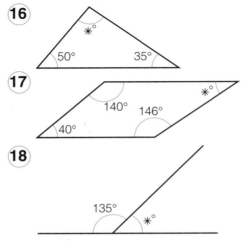

A You need 10 counters.

Place counters on squares with the answers to these questions.
This counter trail will show you that Angus comes from Saturn:
(6×7) (9×3) (2×7) (10×8) (9×9) (5×6) (4×9) (8×5) (4×4) (8×4)

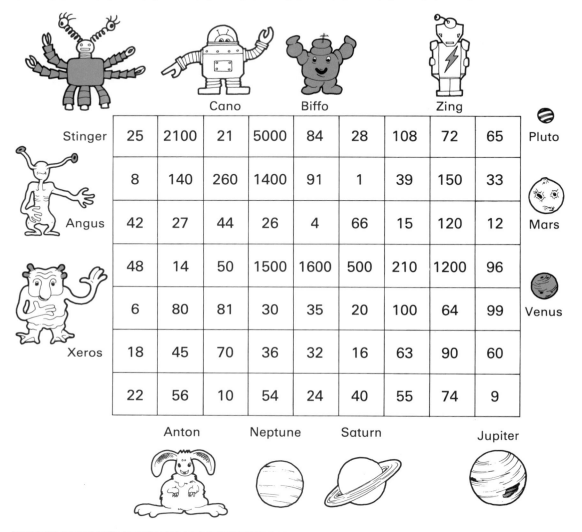

B Place counters on squares with the answers to these sets of
questions. Where does each space person come from?

1 (3×6) (5×9) (10×7) (6×6) (4×8) (7×5) (5×4) (10×10) (8×8) (11×9)

2 (5×5) (4×2) (7×6) (6×8) (7×2) (5×10) (9×9) (7×10) (9×4) (6×9)

3 (8×7) (7×9) (8×2) (2×5) (4×8) (6×10) (6×9) (3×3) (3×8) (10×9)

4 (1×1) (20×6) (14×2) (12×100) (11×6) (50×10) (12×9) (30×7) (3×4) (9×8)

5 (7×3) (1×1) (15×10) (14×100) (13×7) (9×8) (26×10) (13×3) (13×5)

6 (16×100) (10×10) (4×5) (12×7) (8×8) (13×7) (11×9) (2×2) (7×5)

Multiplication

A Write numbers for ✶'s:

☆ 8×5=✶ 40

1	2×7=✶	11	✶×4=16
2	6×5=✶	12	✶×8=56
3	5×7=✶	13	9×9=✶
4	3×8=✶	14	10×10=✶
5	9×4=✶	15	✶×2=20
6	8×6=✶	16	3×9=✶
7	4×✶=32	17	8×4=✶
8	5×✶=40	18	9×✶=54
9	9×✶=45	19	8×✶=64
10	10×✶=70	20	✶×9=27

B Copy and complete:

```
☆      4 2 3          4 2 3
    ×      6       ×      6
    ───────          2 5 3 8
```

```
1      4 5 3      7      2 4 9
    ×      3          ×      9
```

```
2      5 2 3      8      2 6 7
    ×      4          ×      7
```

```
3      6 1 2      9      3 0 7
    ×      5          ×      6
```

```
4      1 5 7     10      1 6 0
    ×      8          ×      9
```

```
5      2 4 5     11      8 0 5
    ×      5          ×      7
```

```
6      8 1 7     12      7 0 0
    ×      2          ×      5
```

C Write answers only:

☆ 61×10=✶ 610

1	42×10=✶	6	193×10=✶
2	51×10=✶	7	264×10=✶
3	77×10=✶	8	177×10=✶
4	80×10=✶	9	333×10=✶
5	65×10=✶	10	702×10=✶

D What is the product of:

☆ 18 and 6?

```
     1 8
  ×    6
  ─────
   1 0 8
```

1	19 and 3?	5	21 and 9?
2	26 and 6?	6	33 and 5?
3	42 and 5?	7	46 and 8?
4	64 and 7?	8	37 and 4?

E Write the factors of:

☆ 15   1 ; 3 ; 5 ; 15

1	22	5	36
2	30	6	24
3	16	7	48
4	28	8	20

F Copy and complete this multiplication square:

×	4	7	8	9
3	12			
5				
6		42		
10				

Multiply 1642 by 4:
$$\begin{array}{r} 1642 \\ \times\quad 4 \\ \hline 6568 \\ \hline {\scriptstyle 2\ 1} \end{array}$$

Multiply 2379 by 3:
$$\begin{array}{r} 2379 \\ \times\quad 3 \\ \hline 7137 \\ \hline {\scriptstyle 1\ 2\ 2} \end{array}$$

A Copy and complete:

☆ 1 4 0 7
× 6
= 8442

1   2 4 5 3
× 4

2   1 0 6 9
× 7

3   1 4 7 2
× 5

4   2 3 9 1
× 3

5   1 3 7 7
× 6

6   1 0 0 9
× 9

7   1 6 0 6
× 5

8   2 4 9 6
× 4

9   3 2 6 7
× 2

10   1 4 7 6
× 6

11   2 0 7 6
× 4

12   1 1 7 7
× 8

B Answer these questions:

☆ There are 1286 seats in a theatre. How many people can be seated for 5 shows.
$$\begin{array}{r} 1286 \\ \times\quad 5 \\ \hline 6430 \end{array}$$

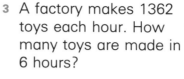

1 What is the total price of 3 boats, each costing £1984?

2 A circus has 1850 seats. If all the seats are booked for 5 evenings, how many tickets are sold altogether?

3 A factory makes 1362 toys each hour. How many toys are made in 6 hours?

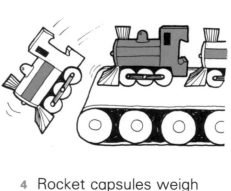

4 Rocket capsules weigh 1468 kilograms. What is the total weight of 4 capsules?

5 Lorries have 6 wheels. How many wheels are needed for 2126 lorries?

6 Steel girders weigh 1198 kilograms. What is the total weight of 8 girders?

Multiplication

Boxes contain 18 biscuits:

CRUMBLE BISCUITS

How many biscuits in 12 boxes?

In **10** boxes there are:
(18×10) biscuits
=**180** biscuits.

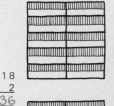

$$\begin{array}{r} 18 \\ \times\ 2 \\ \hline 36 \end{array}$$

In **2** boxes there are:
(18×2) biscuits
=**36** biscuits.

So in **12** boxes there are:
180+36 biscuits=**216 biscuits**.

Write: **18×12=(18×10)+(18×2)**
= 180 + 36
= **216**

A Copy and complete:

☆ 19×13=(19×10)+(19×3)   (19×10)+(19×3)
= **✳** + **✳** = 190 + 57
= **✳**   =   247

1 17×14=(17×10)+(17×4)
= **✳** + **✳**
= **✳**

2 15×13=(15×10)+(15×3)
= **✳** + **✳**
= **✳**

3 19×12=(19×10)+(19×2)
= **✳** + **✳**
= **✳**

4 18×15=(18×10)+(18×5)
= **✳** + **✳**
= **✳**

5 16×16=(16×10)+(16×6)
= **✳** + **✳**
= **✳**

6 14×17=(14×10)+(14×7)
= **✳** + **✳**
= **✳**

Multiply 24 by 13:
24×13=(24×**10**)+(24×**3**)
= 240 + 72
=   312

$$\begin{array}{r} 24 \\ \times\ 3 \\ \hline 72 \end{array}$$

B Work out the answers to these:

☆ 32×14=**✳**   (32×10)+(32×4)
= 320 + 128
=   448

1 18×13=**✳**   6 32×15=**✳**
2 14×12=**✳**   7 31×17=**✳**
3 22×16=**✳**   8 26×12=**✳**
4 24×15=**✳**   9 18×16=**✳**
5 21×17=**✳**   10 34×13=**✳**

C Work out the answers to these:

☆ In a theatre 18 people   18×17
sit in each row. How   = (18×10)+(18×7)
many people can sit   = 180 + 126
in 17 rows?   =   306

1 Chairs cost £16 each. What would be the cost of 18 chairs?

2 A car can travel 12 kilometres using 1 litre of petrol. How far can the car travel using 19 litres of petrol?

3 A lorry can carry 22 crates. How many crates can it carry in 17 loads?

4 There are 34 sweets in each bag. How many sweets are there in 16 bags?

5 A railway carriage holds 45 people. How many people can travel in 18 carriages?

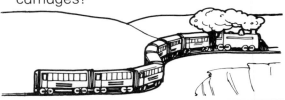

There are 16 chocolates in a box.
How many chocolates are there
in 12 boxes?

We can answer this
question by using
long multiplication:

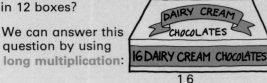

16 DAIRY CREAM CHOCOLATES

```
      1 6
   ×  1 2
```
first multiply 16 by **10:** 160
then multiply 16 by **2:**   32
add: 192

There are **192** chocolates in 12 boxes.

A Write answers to these **long
multiplication** questions:

☆
```
      1 2 5          1 2 5
   ×    1 5       ×    1 5
    1 2 5 0        1 2 5 0  (125×10)
      6 2 5          6 2 5  (125×5)
   ****            1 8 7 5
```

1
```
      3 1
   ×  1 6
    3 1 0  (31×10)
    1 8 6  (31×6)
   ***
```

4
```
      2 4 6
   ×    1 7
    2 4 6 0  (246×10)
    1 7 2 2  (246×7)
   ****
```

2
```
      2 5
   ×  1 6
    2 5 0  (25×10)
    1 5 0  (25×6)
   ***
```

5
```
      3 3 9
   ×    1 8
    3 3 9 0  (339×10)
    2 7 1 2  (339×8)
   ****
```

3
```
      3 5
   ×  1 4
    3 5 0  (35×10)
    1 4 0  (35×4)
   ***
```

6
```
      1 8 8
   ×    1 9
    1 8 8 0  (188×10)
    1 6 9 2  (188×9)
   ****
```

B Copy and complete:

☆
```
      4 3          4 3
   ×  1 6       ×  1 6
   ***          4 3 0
    2 5 8        2 5 8
    6 8 8        6 8 8
```

1
```
      2 8
   ×  1 2
   ***
      5 6
    3 3 6
```

3
```
      2 7
   ×  1 3
    2 7 0
     **
    3 5 1
```

5
```
      1 2 3
   ×    1 4
   ****
      4 9 2
    1 7 2 2
```

2
```
      3 4
   ×  1 5
   ***
    1 7 0
    5 1 0
```

4
```
      4 3
   ×  1 6
    4 3 0
   ***
    6 8 8
```

6
```
      2 4 9
   ×    1 3
    2 4 9 0
     ***
    3 2 3 7
```

C Use **long multiplication** to answer
these:

☆
```
      3 5          3 5
   ×  1 4       ×  1 4
   ***          3 5 0
   ***          1 4 0
   ***          4 9 0
```

1
```
      4 1
   ×  1 2
   ***
    **
   ***
```

3
```
      2 6
   ×  1 5
   ***
   ***
   ***
```

5
```
      1 2 6
   ×    1 4
   ****
    ***
   ****
```

2
```
      3 5
   ×  1 4
   ***
   ***
   ***
```

4
```
      3 7
   ×  1 8
   ***
   ***
   ***
```

6
```
      2 4 7
   ×    1 7
   ****
   ****
   ****
```

Multiplication

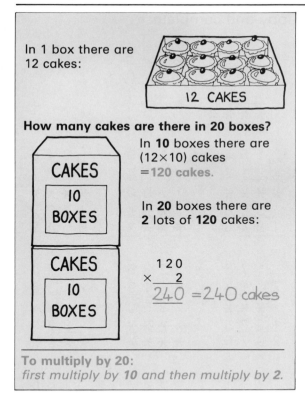

In 1 box there are 12 cakes:

12 CAKES

How many cakes are there in 20 boxes?

CAKES
10 BOXES

CAKES
10 BOXES

In **10** boxes there are (12×10) cakes
=**120 cakes**.

In **20** boxes there are **2** lots of **120** cakes:

$$\begin{array}{r} 1\,2\,0 \\ \times2 \\ \hline 240 \end{array} = 240 \text{ cakes}$$

To multiply by 20:
first multiply by 10 and then multiply by 2.

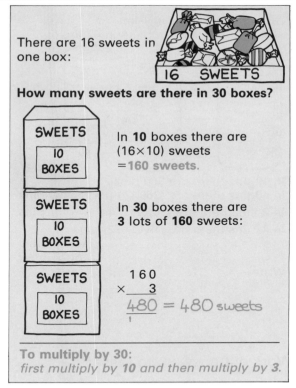

There are 16 sweets in one box:

16 SWEETS

How many sweets are there in 30 boxes?

SWEETS
10 BOXES

SWEETS
10 BOXES

SWEETS
10 BOXES

In **10** boxes there are (16×10) sweets
=**160 sweets**.

In **30** boxes there are **3** lots of **160** sweets:

$$\begin{array}{r} 1\,6\,0 \\ \times3 \\ \hline 480 \end{array} = 480 \text{ sweets}$$

To multiply by 30:
first multiply by 10 and then multiply by 3.

A Write answers only:

☆ 36×10= ✶ 360

1 17×10= ✶
2 23×10= ✶
3 45×10= ✶
4 56×10= ✶
5 20×10= ✶

6 40×10= ✶
7 84×10= ✶
8 67×10= ✶
9 94×10= ✶
10 99×10= ✶

B Work out answers for these:

☆ 24×20= ✶
24×10 = 240

$$\begin{array}{r} 240 \\ \times2 \\ \hline 480 \end{array}$$

1 16×20= ✶
2 31×20= ✶
3 25×20= ✶
4 63×20= ✶
5 70×20= ✶

6 38×20= ✶
7 46×20= ✶
8 57×20= ✶
9 65×20= ✶
10 96×20= ✶

C Copy and complete:

☆ To multiply by 50, first multiply by ✶ and then multiply by ✶.

To multiply by 50, first multiply by 10 and then multiply by 5

1 To multiply by 40, first multiply by ✶ and then multiply by ✶.
2 To multiply by 60, first multiply by ✶ and then multiply by ✶.
3 To multiply by 80, first multiply by ✶ and then multiply by ✶.

D Work out answers for these:

☆ 28×70= ✶
28×10 = 280

$$\begin{array}{r} 280 \\ \times7 \\ \hline 1960 \end{array}$$

1 23×30= ✶
2 52×30= ✶
3 41×40= ✶
4 53×50= ✶

5 60×30= ✶
6 70×80= ✶
7 54×70= ✶
8 68×90= ✶

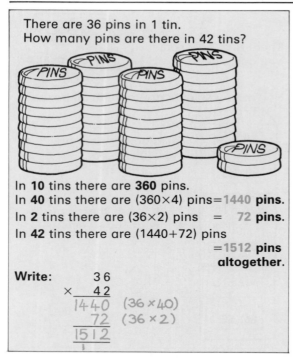

There are 36 pins in 1 tin.
How many pins are there in 42 tins?

In **10** tins there are **360** pins.
In **40** tins there are (360×4) pins=**1440** **pins**.
In **2** tins there are (36×2) pins = **72** **pins**.
In **42** tins there are (1440+72) pins
                                              =**1512** **pins**
                                              altogether.

Write: 3 6
           ×   4 2
           1440   (36×40)
             72   (36×2)
           1512

A Work out answers to these:

☆ 1 box contains
   28 crackers.
   How many
   crackers
   in 26 boxes?

       28
    × 26
      560   (28×20)
      168   (28×6)
      728

1 There are 28 tins in a
  box. How many tins are
  there in 24 boxes?

28 TINS

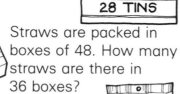

2 Straws are packed in
  boxes of 48. How many
  straws are there in
  36 boxes?

3 Balloons are sold in
  bags of 32. How many
  balloons in 28 bags?

4 There are 37 fireworks
  in a box. How many
  fireworks are there in
  52 boxes?

B Copy and complete:

☆   1 3 7   1 3 7
      ×   2 3   ×   2 3
      * * * *   2 7 4 0
        4 1 1   4 1 1
      * * * *   3 1 5 1

1   1 5 4   4   1 7 9   7   2 4 6
    ×   1 2   ×   1 4   ×   2 7
    * * * *   1 7 9 0   * * * *
      3 0 8   * * *   1 7 2 2
    1 8 4 8   * * * *   6 6 4 2

2   1 7 5   5   2 3 5   8   1 7 4
    ×   1 7   ×   1 9   ×   3 5
    * * * *   2 3 5 0   * * * *
    1 2 2 5   * * * *   8 7 0
    2 9 7 5   * * * *   * * * *

3   2 3 1   6   3 2 7   9   1 8 6
    ×   1 4   ×   2 4   ×   4 6
    2 3 1 0   6 5 4 0   7 4 4 0
    * * *   * * * *   * * * *
    3 2 3 4   7 8 4 8   * * * *

C **Use long multiplication** to answer
these:

☆ School tables   £ 2 7
  cost £27.   ×   3 4
  What is the   8 1 0
  cost of 34 tables?   1 0 8
                          £ 9 1 8

1 A school journey costs £35 for each
  child. What is the total cost for 28
  children?

2 There are 144 nails in a box. How
  many nails are there in 36 boxes?

3 There are 32 pieces in a chess set.
  How many pieces in 43 chess sets?

4 There are 168 hours in a week. How
  many hours are there in 52 weeks?

Multiplication

This machine gives pennies for £1 coins.

A How many pennies will the machine give for these amounts?

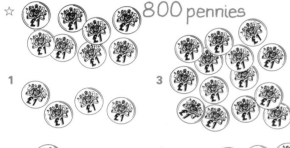

☆ 800 pennies

1
2
3
4

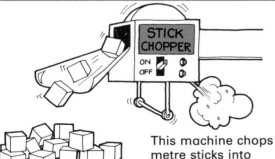

STICK CHOPPER
ON
OFF

This machine chops metre sticks into centimetre pieces.

B How many centimetre pieces will the machine make from:

☆ 5 metre sticks? 500

1 6 metre sticks?
2 9 metre sticks?
3 7 metre sticks?
4 11 metre sticks?
5 13 metre sticks?

6 15 metre sticks?
7 19 metre sticks?
8 14 metre sticks?
9 20 metre sticks?
10 22 metre sticks?

To **multiply** a number by **100**, move the number **2 columns to the left**:

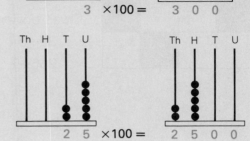

3 ×100 = 3 0 0

2 5 ×100 = 2 5 0 0

C **Multiply by 100** the number shown on each abacus. Draw an abacus to show your answer:

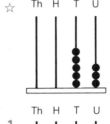 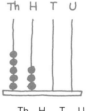

☆

1 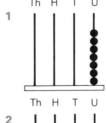   3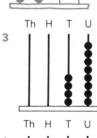

2 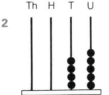   4

D Write answers only:

☆ 29×100=✱ 2900

1 6×100=✱
2 9×100=✱
3 15×100=✱
4 28×100=✱

5 47×100=✱
6 39×100=✱
7 88×100=✱
8 70×100=✱

You need some centimetre squared paper.
Copy and complete these number crosswords:

A

Clues across:
- 1 60÷4
- 4 27÷9
- 5 272÷8
- 6 240÷5
- 7 243÷9
- 8 90÷10

Clues down:
- 1 39÷3
- 2 25÷5
- 3 84÷6
- 5 266÷7
- 6 282÷6
- 8 81÷9

B Clues across:
- 1 312÷6
- 3 246÷3
- 5 36÷9
- 7 72÷8
- 8 628÷4
- 10 54÷6
- 11 20÷5
- 13 276÷6
- 15 261÷3

Clues down:
- 1 378÷7
- 2 20÷10
- 4 232÷8
- 6 770÷5
- 9 56÷8
- 10 752÷8
- 12 259÷7
- 14 36÷6
- 15 72÷9

C

Clues across:
- 1 486÷9
- 3 1113÷7
- 6 2155÷5
- 8 408÷6
- 9 705÷3
- 11 952÷7
- 13 504÷9
- 14 3408÷8
- 16 1635÷5
- 17 450÷9

Clues down:
- 1 3276÷6
- 2 172÷4
- 4 2825÷5
- 5 882÷9
- 7 984÷8
- 10 3276÷9
- 11 1134÷7
- 12 2300÷5
- 13 265÷5
- 15 225÷9

When you put 100 pennies
into this machine,
it gives you a pound coin.

A How many pound
coins does the
machine give when
you put in:

☆ 1300 pennies? 13

1 600 pennies?	6 1200 pennies?
2 900 pennies?	7 1800 pennies?
3 500 pennies?	8 1600 pennies?
4 800 pennies?	9 2000 pennies?
5 1000 pennies?	10 2300 pennies?

This tea machine puts 100 g of tea in each packet.

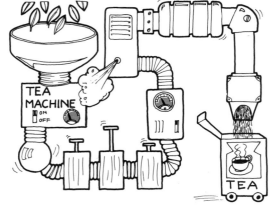

B How many packets can be filled with:

☆ 1700 g of tea? 17

1 200 g of tea?	6 1900 g of tea?
2 700 g of tea?	7 2100 g of tea?
3 400 g of tea?	8 2800 g of tea?
4 1100 g of tea?	9 3000 g of tea?
5 1500 g of tea?	10 3600 g of tea?

To **divide** a number by **100**, move the
number **2 columns to the right**:

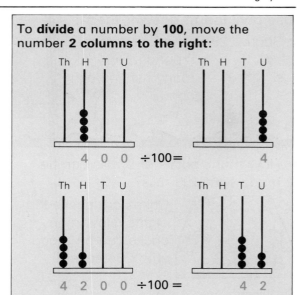

4 0 0 ÷100 = 4

4 2 0 0 ÷100 = 4 2

C **Divide by 100** the number shown on
each abacus. Draw an abacus to
show your answer:

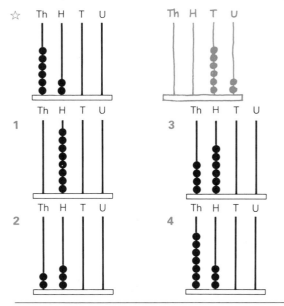

D Write answers only:

☆ 3800÷100= ✳ 38

1 700÷100= ✳	5 2900÷100= ✳
2 900÷100= ✳	6 3200÷100= ✳
3 1800÷100= ✳	7 7200÷100= ✳
4 2000÷100= ✳	8 9900÷100= ✳

A Use **division** to answer these:

☆ Share 225 fish equally among 5 ponds. How many fish in each pond?

$$5\overline{)225} \quad 45$$

Divide 7555 by 5:

$$5\overline{)7555} \quad 1511$$

Divide 5628 by 4:

$$4\overline{)5628} \quad 1407$$

1 How many packs of 9 rolls can be made with 108 rolls?

2
Cakes are packed in eights. How many packs can be made with 264 cakes?

8 CAKES

3 $4\overline{)748}$

4 Harry eats $\frac{1}{6}$ of a packet of sweets. If there were 42 sweets in the packet, how many did Harry eat?

5 How many is $\frac{1}{8}$ of 112?

6 $7430 \div 10$

7 How many each and how many left over when 387 stamps are shared equally among 7 children?

8 $7\overline{)644}$

9 994 ml of water fills a jug twice. How much does the jug hold?

10 How much is $\frac{1}{4}$ of £684?

11
How many diaries are left over when 427 diaries are packed in boxes of 6?

B Copy and complete:

☆ $8\overline{)6352} \quad 794$

1 $6\overline{)8406}$

2 $3\overline{)6216}$

3 $4\overline{)2320}$

4 $7\overline{)1428}$

5 $5\overline{)6150}$

6 $8\overline{)7152}$

7 $9\overline{)9324}$

8 $6\overline{)8214}$

C Answer these questions:

☆ 5 people are given an equal share of £7250. How much does each person receive?

$$5\overline{)£7250} \quad £1450$$

1 A bakery packs 8 cakes in a tray. How many trays will be needed for 2696 cakes?

2 A metal beam weighs 4266 kg. What is half the weight of the beam?

3 6853 seats can be booked for 7 performances of a pantomime. How many seats can be booked for each performance?

4 How many bags of 9 oranges can be made with 1287 oranges?

Revision for pages 29–40

A Write numbers for *'s:

1 6×9=*
2 5×7=*
3 9×8=*
4 10×7=*
5 8×6=*
6 7×7=*
7 5×9=*
8 8×8=*
9 9×9=*
10 4×8=*

B What are the **factors** of:

1 12?
2 16?
3 20?
4 32?
5 36?
6 30?
7 48?
8 18?
9 28?

C Copy and complete:

1 $\begin{array}{r} 427 \\ \times\quad 5 \\ \hline \end{array}$

2 $\begin{array}{r} 209 \\ \times\quad 7 \\ \hline \end{array}$

3 $\begin{array}{r} 437 \\ \times\quad 8 \\ \hline \end{array}$

4 $\begin{array}{r} 365 \\ \times\quad 6 \\ \hline \end{array}$

5 $\begin{array}{r} 429 \\ \times\quad 3 \\ \hline \end{array}$

6 $\begin{array}{r} 1271 \\ \times\quad 6 \\ \hline \end{array}$

7 $\begin{array}{r} 2429 \\ \times\quad 3 \\ \hline \end{array}$

8 $\begin{array}{r} 1338 \\ \times\quad 7 \\ \hline \end{array}$

9 $\begin{array}{r} 2137 \\ \times\quad 4 \\ \hline \end{array}$

10 $\begin{array}{r} 3073 \\ \times\quad 3 \\ \hline \end{array}$

D Work out the **product** of:

1 37 and 6
2 24 and 8
3 47 and 10
4 56 and 5
5 49 and 7
6 54 and 9
7 43 and 20
8 32 and 30
9 26 and 40
10 35 and 50

E Copy and complete:

1 $\begin{array}{r} 26 \\ \times\quad 17 \\ \hline *** \\ *** \\ \hline *** \end{array}$

2 $\begin{array}{r} 37 \\ \times\quad 15 \\ \hline *** \\ *** \\ \hline *** \end{array}$

3 $\begin{array}{r} 52 \\ \times\quad 18 \\ \hline *** \\ *** \\ \hline *** \end{array}$

4 $\begin{array}{r} 182 \\ \times\quad 13 \\ \hline **** \\ *** \\ \hline **** \end{array}$

5 $\begin{array}{r} 165 \\ \times\quad 14 \\ \hline **** \\ *** \\ \hline **** \end{array}$

6 $\begin{array}{r} 261 \\ \times\quad 29 \\ \hline **** \\ **** \\ \hline **** \end{array}$

7 $\begin{array}{r} 328 \\ \times\quad 36 \\ \hline **** \\ **** \\ \hline **** \end{array}$

8 $\begin{array}{r} 247 \\ \times\quad 41 \\ \hline **** \\ *** \\ \hline **** \end{array}$

F Write answers only:

1 7×100=*
2 52×10=*
3 64×100=*
4 21×10=*
5 46×100=*
6 4600÷100=*
7 870÷10=*
8 3100÷100=*
9 6000÷100=*
10 3000÷10=*

G Copy and complete:

1 $8\overline{)4704}$
2 $5\overline{)3945}$
3 $7\overline{)4606}$
4 $9\overline{)4077}$
5 $4\overline{)8928}$
6 $6\overline{)3048}$
7 $3\overline{)2961}$
8 $8\overline{)4104}$

A Here is a quick check for multiplication problems.

Find the digital roots of the 2 numbers.

$$
\begin{array}{r}
4\,2\,6 \\
\times \quad 5 \\
\hline
2\,1\,3\,0
\end{array}
$$

4 + 2 + 6 = 12   1 + 2 = **3**

.... **5**

Multiply the two digital roots together:

3 × 5 = 15

Find the digital root of the new number: **1** + **5** = **6**

Find the digital root of the answer: **2** + **1** + **3** + **0** = **6**

If these 2 digital roots are the same your answer is likely to be correct. If they are different your answer is certainly wrong.

Try this answer check for these problems:
a) **818** × **7**   b) **239** × **5**   c) **1024** × **8**   d) **36** × **18**

Try this method for 5 questions of your own.

B Using only the number 7 and the signs + − × ÷ how many of the numbers up to 100 can you produce on a calculator?

Example: 10 = (77 − 7) ÷ 7

Investigate and continue this pattern:

5 × 7 = ✳   55 × 7 = ✳   555 × 7 = ✳

Write any 2-digit number and repeat it twice.

Example: 676767. Is this number a multiple of 7?
Investigate if this is true for other 2–digit numbers.

C Work out all of the prime numbers less than 100.

Choose any even number larger than 6 but less than 200.
Can you find 2 prime numbers that can be added together to make your even number?

Repeat this investigation for 10 other even numbers between 6 and 200.

Choose any odd number between 6 and 200.
Can you find 3 prime numbers that can be added together to make your odd number?

Repeat this investigation for 10 other odd numbers between 6 and 200.

Answer any questions you can. Leave those you cannot do.

1 9 × 5 = ✱

2 7 × 8 = ✱

3 6 × ✱ = 42

4 Write 2 numbers that make this multiplication problem correct:

✱ × ✱ = 63

5 1 3
× 5

6 9 1 2
×   5

7 84 is a multiple of 7. True or false?

Write the product of:

8 8 and 5

9 28 and 4

10 113 and 5

11 Write the factors of 27.

12 Write the factors of 25.

13 Write a number between 41 and 50 that has 4 and 8 as factors.

14 12 × 10 = ✱

15 52 × 10 = ✱

16 165 × 10 = ✱

17 19 × 100 = ✱

18 ✱ × 100 = 6500

19 1 4 3 7
×   4

20 1 2 3 8
×   9

21 2 5 ✱
Write a figure that makes this number a multiple of 5.

22 A taxi can carry 8 people. How many taxis would be needed to transport 1496 people?

23   5 7
× 1 6

24 2 3 4
× 1 8

25 53 × 20 = ✱

26 42 × 50 = ✱

27 68 × 1000 = ✱

28 126 × 1000 = ✱

29 18 ÷ 3 = ✱

30 80 ÷ 10 = ✱

31 ✱ ÷ 10 = 29

32 3200 ÷ 100 = ✱

33 29 000 ÷ 1000 = ✱

34 How many each and how many left over when 286 buns are shared equally among 8 elephants?

35 How much is $\frac{1}{8}$ of £904?

36 6 ⟌ 84

37 8 ⟌ 592

38 7 ⟌ 1869

39

1068 seats can be booked for 6 performances of a play. How many seats can be booked for each performance?

A Write these dates in figures:

☆ 26th November 1982   26.11.82

1   14th June 1981

2   24th September 1969

3   12th February 1974

4   16th December 1951

5   6th June 1980

6   28th May 1944

7   20th January 1983

8   15th April 1966

9   1st October 1973

10   29th February 1976

B Write these times in figures:

☆ 25 past 4   4.25

1 10 past 9	5 half past 11
2 20 past 6	6 quarter to 12
3 25 to 3	7 20 to 5
4 10 to 1	8 5 to 7

C Write these times in 2 different ways:

☆    23 minutes past 2
2.23

1    4

2   5

3   6

D What time will it be 20 minutes after these morning times?

☆ 6.23 am   6.43 am

1 8.25 am	5 4.40 am	9 9.57 am
2 11.16 am	6 3.08 am	10 10.49 am
3 1.25 am	7 5.45 am	11 7.55 am
4 2.36 am	8 6.50 am	12 2.58 am

E What time will it be 15 minutes before these afternoon times?

☆ 3.41 pm   3.26 pm

1 8.45 pm	5 7.16 pm	9 3.05 pm
2 6.30 pm	6 9.15 pm	10 4.12 pm
3 2.27 pm	7 6.31 pm	11 1.06 pm
4 8.56 pm	8 10.10 pm	12 11.01 pm

F Write the time that is:

☆ 8 minutes later than 4.27 pm   4.35 pm

1   7 minutes earlier than 5.42 am

2   16 minutes later than 8.02 pm

3   23 minutes after 6.35 pm

4   29 minutes before 8.15 pm

5   24 minutes after 10.53 am

G How long do these journeys take?

	start time	finish time	
☆	8.43 am	9.15 am	32 minutes
1	6.27 pm	6.41 pm	
2	9.27 am	10.08 pm	
3	6.43 pm	8.12 pm	
4	1.26 pm	3.50 pm	
5	8.46 am	10.37 pm	
6	5.38 pm	8.07 pm	
7	9.26 pm	11.52 pm	
8	4.32 pm	8.22 pm	

Time

 This watch shows the time 4.18.

But the watch is 8 minutes *slow*.

The correct time is 4.26.

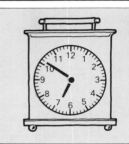 This clock shows the time 6.51.

But the clock is 11 minutes *fast*.

The correct time is 6.40.

A Write the correct times for these clocks and watches:

☆ 6 minutes *slow*

 7.34

1

7 minutes *slow*

4

30 minutes *slow*

2

9 minutes *slow*

5

$\frac{1}{4}$ hour *slow*

3

11 minutes *slow*

6

$\frac{3}{4}$ hour *slow*

B Write the correct times for these clocks and watches:

☆ 12 minutes *fast*

 4.43

1

10 minutes *fast*

4

25 minutes *fast*

2

8 minutes *fast*

5

$\frac{3}{4}$ hour *fast*

3

22 minutes *fast*

6

$1\frac{1}{2}$ hours *fast*

Digital clocks and watches show
24-hour clock times.
Four figures are shown.

The first 2 figures show the number of hours after Midnight.

The last 2 figures show the number of minutes past the hour.

This time is 11.34 am.
6.00 am is written as 06.00
10.05 am is written as 10.05
2.00 pm is written as 14.00
8.45 pm is written as 20.45

At Midnight digital clocks show 00.00.
12.15 am is shown as 00.15.

B Write these times as **24-hour clock** times:

☆ 12.26 am   00.26

1	12.24 am	6	12.26 pm
2	12.37 am	7	12.41 pm
3	12.54 am	8	12.15 am
4	12.39 am	9	Noon
5	Midnight	10	12.12 am

A Copy and complete:

	am or pm time	24-hour clock time
☆	9.52 pm	21.52
1	4.20 am	
2	6.30 am	
3	11.22 am	
4	7.51 am	
5	6.42 am	
6	3.36 am	
7	1.00 pm	
8	5.00 pm	
9	11.00 pm	
10	7.00 pm	
11	6.52 pm	
12	4.12 pm	
13	10.24 pm	
14	6.02 pm	
15	8.06 pm	
16	8.09 am	
17	8.12 pm	
18	9.51 pm	

C Write the times shown on these clocks as **am** or **pm** times:

☆

5.32 pm

Time

A Write the afternoon and evening times below as **24-hour clock** times:

☆  19.05

1

6

2

7

3

8

4

9

5

10

B Write these **24-hour clock** times as am or pm times:

☆ 16.40 4.40 pm

1	11.25	5	19.30	9	17.15
2	10.00	6	14.05	10	23.10
3	09.50	7	22.35	11	04.55
4	15.20	8	16.45	12	07.40

Train time-table				
	train 1	train 2	train 3	train 4
Waterloo	13.52	14.22	14.52	15.22
Esher	14.13	14.43	15.13	15.43
Hersham	14.16	14.46	15.16	15.46
Walton	14.19	14.49	15.19	15.49
Weybridge	14.23	14.53	15.23	15.53
New Haw	14.26	14.56	15.26	15.56
Byfleet	14.29	14.59	15.29	15.59

C Use the train time-table to answer these questions:

☆ How long does train 3 take to travel from Waterloo to New Haw?

34 minutes

1 How long does train 1 take to travel from Esher to Byfleet?

2 How long does train 4 take to travel from Waterloo to Weybridge?

3 How long does train 3 take to travel from Waterloo to Byfleet?

4 If you needed to be in New Haw at 3.30 pm, which train would you catch?

5 If you needed to be in Walton at 3.00 pm, which train would you catch?

6 Has train 1 reached Weybridge when train 2 leaves Waterloo?

7 How long after train 2 reaches Byfleet does train 4 leave Waterloo?

8 Which train would you catch to be in Hersham by 3.10 pm?

9 If you miss the 13.52 train at Waterloo, what is the earliest time you can arrive at Byfleet?

10 If train 4 runs 12 minutes late at what time will it arrive at New Haw?

A Write these dates in figures:

1 3rd January 1983

2 24th September 1976

3 18th October 1980

4 6th June 1974

5 28th May 1981

6 10th July 1970

7 27th November 1972

8 8th August 1981

9 5th February 1983

10 25th December 1955

B Write these times in figures:

1 half past 6   6 quarter past 3

2 25 to 9   7 25 past 2

3 20 past 3   8 5 to 5

4 20 to 7   9 10 to 1

5 10 past 10   10 quarter to 12

C Write the time that is:

1 6 minutes later than 6.27 am

2 9 minutes earlier than 4.36 pm

3 22 minutes later than 12.38 pm

4 17 minutes before 11.21 am

5 33 minutes after 6.40 pm

6 half an hour earlier than 5.10 am

7 quarter of an hour later than 2.55 pm

8 40 minutes later than 11.50 am

D How long do these journeys take?

	start time	finish time
1	2.26 pm	3.10 pm
2	4.17 pm	5.32 pm
3	8.05 am	9.16 am
4	10.10 am	12.02 pm
5	9.45 pm	11.03 pm
6	6.05 am	7.51 am

E Write the correct times for these clocks and watches:

1

8 minutes *slow*

4

18 minutes *fast*

2
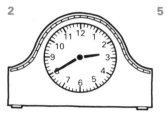
15 minutes *fast*

5

33 minutes *slow*

3

20 minutes *slow*

6

14 minutes *fast*

F Write these times as **24-hour clock** times:

1 7.24 am   5 10.28 pm

2 8.20 pm   6 12.32 am

3 3.51 pm   7 1.05 pm

4 2.16 am   8 8.47 am

G Change these **24-hour clock** times to **am** or **pm** times:

1 16.47   5 21.02

2 10.23   6 12.30

3 07.56   7 19.47

4 14.05   8 22.23

Fractions

A Write numbers for ✻'s:

☆ $\frac{3}{4}=\frac{✻}{8}$ $\frac{3}{4}=\frac{6}{8}$

1 $\frac{1}{2}=\frac{✻}{4}$ 11 $\frac{1}{3}=\frac{✻}{9}$

2 $\frac{1}{3}=\frac{✻}{6}$ 12 $\frac{✻}{8}=\frac{1}{4}$

3 $\frac{1}{4}=\frac{✻}{8}$ 13 $\frac{2}{3}=\frac{✻}{9}$

4 $\frac{1}{5}=\frac{✻}{10}$ 14 $\frac{1}{3}=\frac{4}{✻}$

5 $\frac{1}{6}=\frac{✻}{12}$ 15 $\frac{3}{✻}=\frac{6}{10}$

6 $\frac{2}{5}=\frac{✻}{10}$ 16 $\frac{5}{✻}=\frac{10}{12}$

7 $\frac{3}{4}=\frac{✻}{8}$ 17 $\frac{3}{4}=\frac{6}{✻}$

8 $\frac{3}{5}=\frac{✻}{10}$ 18 $\frac{9}{12}=\frac{3}{✻}$

9 $\frac{5}{6}=\frac{✻}{12}$ 19 $1=\frac{5}{✻}$

10 $\frac{4}{5}=\frac{✻}{10}$ 20 $\frac{7}{✻}=1$

B Copy and complete:

☆ $\frac{3}{5}+\frac{3}{10}=\frac{✻}{10}+\frac{3}{10}=\frac{✻}{✻}$ $\frac{3}{5}+\frac{3}{10}=\frac{6}{10}+\frac{3}{10}=\frac{9}{10}$

1 $\frac{1}{3}+\frac{1}{6}=\frac{✻}{6}+\frac{1}{6}=\frac{✻}{✻}$

2 $\frac{7}{10}+\frac{1}{5}=\frac{7}{10}+\frac{✻}{10}=\frac{✻}{✻}$

3 $\frac{3}{4}+\frac{1}{8}=\frac{✻}{8}+\frac{1}{8}=\frac{✻}{✻}$

4 $\frac{2}{3}+\frac{1}{6}=\frac{✻}{6}+\frac{1}{6}=\frac{✻}{✻}$

5 $\frac{1}{9}+\frac{2}{3}=\frac{1}{9}+\frac{✻}{9}=\frac{✻}{✻}$

6 $\frac{5}{6}+\frac{1}{12}=\frac{✻}{12}+\frac{1}{12}=\frac{✻}{✻}$

7 $\frac{1}{2}+\frac{1}{8}=\frac{4}{✻}+\frac{1}{8}=\frac{✻}{✻}$

8 $\frac{3}{10}+\frac{2}{5}=\frac{3}{10}+\frac{✻}{10}=\frac{✻}{✻}$

9 $\frac{1}{12}+\frac{1}{6}+\frac{1}{3}=\frac{1}{12}+\frac{✻}{12}+\frac{✻}{12}=\frac{✻}{✻}$

10 $\frac{1}{3}+\frac{1}{4}+\frac{1}{12}=\frac{✻}{12}+\frac{✻}{12}+\frac{1}{12}=\frac{✻}{✻}$

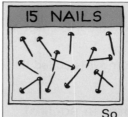

15 NAILS How many nails in $\frac{2}{5}$ of this group?

$\frac{1}{5}$ of the nails is 15÷5=**3**
So $\frac{2}{5}$ of the nails is **3×2=6**

C How many nails in:

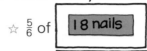

☆ $\frac{5}{6}$ of ⌈18 nails⌉ $\frac{1}{6}$ of the nails = 3
                                $\frac{5}{6}$ of the nails = 15

1 $\frac{3}{8}$ of ⌈24 nails⌉   3 $\frac{5}{8}$ of ⌈40 nails⌉

2 $\frac{2}{9}$ of ⌈27 nails⌉   4 $\frac{7}{10}$ of ⌈30 nails⌉

D How many are:

☆ $\frac{3}{8}$ of 32 sweets? $\frac{1}{8}$ of the sweets = 4
                                $\frac{3}{8}$ of the sweets = 12

1 $\frac{3}{4}$ of 16 cakes?   5 $\frac{5}{7}$ of 35 books?

2 $\frac{3}{5}$ of 20 nuts?   6 $\frac{9}{10}$ of 80 pens?

3 $\frac{2}{9}$ of 36 sweets?   7 $\frac{8}{9}$ of 63 tickets?

4 $\frac{7}{8}$ of 32 toys?   8 $\frac{5}{6}$ of 54 pages?

E Work out these amounts:

☆ $\frac{3}{10}$ of £40 $\frac{1}{10}$ of £40 = £4
                          $\frac{3}{10}$ of £40 = £12

1 $\frac{2}{5}$ of £30   6 $\frac{5}{5}$ of £35

2 $\frac{3}{4}$ of £40   7 $\frac{4}{9}$ of £45

3 $\frac{5}{8}$ of £48   8 $\frac{11}{12}$ of £36

4 $\frac{5}{6}$ of £48   9 $\frac{3}{5}$ of £55

5 $\frac{2}{7}$ of £42   10 $\frac{3}{8}$ of £96

In a fraction, the top number is called the numerator ⟶ $\dfrac{3}{4}$

the bottom number is called the denominator ⟶

A Double the **denominator** in each of these fractions:

☆ $\frac{2}{3}$ $\frac{2}{6}$

1 $\frac{1}{5}$ 3 $\frac{1}{7}$ 5 $\frac{5}{6}$

2 $\frac{3}{4}$ 4 $\frac{3}{10}$ 6 $\frac{7}{8}$

B Double the **numerator** in each of these fractions:

☆ $\frac{1}{3}$ $\frac{2}{3}$

1 $\frac{1}{5}$ 3 $\frac{1}{6}$ 5 $\frac{3}{10}$

2 $\frac{2}{7}$ 4 $\frac{4}{9}$ 6 $\frac{7}{8}$

C Double both the **numerator** and **denominator** in these fractions:

☆ $\frac{2}{5}$ $\frac{4}{10}$

1 $\frac{1}{4}$ 3 $\frac{2}{5}$ 5 $\frac{3}{8}$

2 $\frac{1}{3}$ 4 $\frac{3}{4}$ 6 $\frac{5}{6}$

D Does a fraction become larger, smaller or stay the same size when you:

1 double the denominator?

2 double the numerator?

3 double both numerator and denominator?

4 treble both numerator and denominator?

5 multiply both numerator and denominator by 4?

6 multiply both numerator and denominator by 10?

E Copy and complete:

$\frac{1}{2} = \frac{\textbf{*}}{4} = \frac{\textbf{*}}{6} = \frac{\textbf{*}}{8} = \frac{5}{\textbf{*}}$

$\frac{1}{2} = \frac{2}{4} = \frac{3}{6} = \frac{4}{8} = \frac{5}{10}$

1 $\frac{1}{3} = \frac{\textbf{*}}{6} = \frac{\textbf{*}}{9} = \frac{4}{\textbf{*}}$

2 $\frac{1}{4} = \frac{\textbf{*}}{8} = \frac{\textbf{*}}{12} = \frac{\textbf{*}}{20} = \frac{\textbf{*}}{40}$

3 $\frac{1}{5} = \frac{\textbf{*}}{10} = \frac{3}{\textbf{*}} = \frac{\textbf{*}}{20} = \frac{\textbf{*}}{40}$

4 $\frac{2}{3} = \frac{\textbf{*}}{6} = \frac{\textbf{*}}{9} = \frac{\textbf{*}}{12} = \frac{\textbf{*}}{15}$

5 $\frac{2}{5} = \frac{4}{\textbf{*}} = \frac{6}{\textbf{*}} = \frac{8}{\textbf{*}}$

6 $\frac{5}{6} = \frac{\textbf{*}}{12} = \frac{15}{\textbf{*}}$

7 $\frac{3}{4} = \frac{\textbf{*}}{8} = \frac{9}{\textbf{*}} = \frac{\textbf{*}}{24}$

8 $\frac{4}{5} = \frac{\textbf{*}}{10} = \frac{16}{\textbf{*}} = \frac{\textbf{*}}{40}$

F Rewrite these fractions so that they have the same **denominator**:

☆ $\frac{3}{4}$; $\frac{2}{3}$ (change to twelfths) $\frac{9}{12}$; $\frac{8}{12}$

1 $\frac{1}{2}$; $\frac{1}{4}$ (change to quarters)

2 $\frac{1}{2}$; $\frac{1}{3}$ (change to sixths)

3 $\frac{1}{4}$; $\frac{1}{3}$ (change to twelfths)

4 $\frac{2}{3}$; $\frac{3}{4}$ (change to twelfths)

5 $\frac{2}{5}$; $\frac{1}{2}$ (change to tenths)

6 $\frac{1}{2}$; $\frac{2}{3}$ (change to sixths)

7 $\frac{4}{5}$; $\frac{2}{3}$ (change to fifteenths)

8 $\frac{1}{10}$; $\frac{1}{4}$ (change to twentieths)

9 $\frac{5}{6}$; $\frac{3}{4}$ (change to twelfths)

10 $\frac{1}{6}$; $\frac{2}{9}$ (change to eighteenths)

Fractions

 1 whole=4 quarters
Write: $1=\frac{4}{4}$

 2 whole ones=8 quarters
Write: $2=\frac{8}{4}$

 $3=\frac{12}{4}$

A fraction that has a numerator larger than the denominator is called an **improper fraction**:

$\frac{12}{4}$ is an **improper fraction**.

A number that has whole ones **and** a fraction is called a **mixed number**:

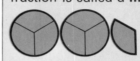

Say:
'two and one-third'
Write: $2\frac{1}{3}$

You can change a **mixed number** to an **improper fraction**:

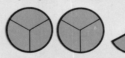

3 thirds+3 thirds+1 third=7 thirds=$\frac{7}{3}$

$2\frac{1}{3}=\frac{7}{3}$

A Copy and complete:

☆ $2=\frac{*}{3}$ $2=\frac{6}{3}$

1 $3=\frac{*}{5}$

2 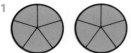 $2=\frac{*}{8}$

3 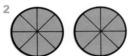 $3=\frac{*}{10}$

B Write these numbers as **improper fractions**:

☆ $3=\frac{*}{8}$ $3=\frac{24}{8}$

1 $2=\frac{*}{5}$ **4** $3=\frac{*}{4}$ **7** $3=\frac{*}{9}$

2 $2=\frac{*}{10}$ **5** $4=\frac{*}{2}$ **8** $4=\frac{*}{10}$

3 $3=\frac{*}{6}$ **6** $2=\frac{*}{7}$ **9** $5=\frac{*}{6}$

C Write these improper fractions as whole numbers:

☆ $\frac{18}{6}=*$ 3

1 $\frac{12}{4}=*$ **4** $\frac{20}{10}=*$ **7** $\frac{24}{6}=*$

2 $\frac{15}{5}=*$ **5** $\frac{30}{6}=*$ **8** $\frac{50}{10}=*$

3 $\frac{12}{3}=*$ **6** $\frac{30}{5}=*$ **9** $\frac{32}{4}=*$

D Change these **mixed numbers** to **improper fractions**:

☆ 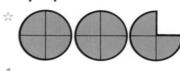 $2\frac{3}{4}=\frac{*}{4}$

$2\frac{3}{4}=\frac{11}{4}$

1 $2\frac{1}{5}=\frac{*}{5}$

2 $3\frac{3}{10}=\frac{*}{10}$

3 $3\frac{5}{6}=\frac{*}{6}$

4 $2\frac{7}{8}=\frac{*}{8}$

E Change these **mixed numbers** to **improper fractions**:

☆ $4\frac{1}{3}=\frac{*}{3}$ $4\frac{1}{3}=\frac{13}{3}$

1 $2\frac{1}{6}=\frac{*}{6}$ **4** $5\frac{1}{4}=\frac{*}{4}$ **7** $2\frac{2}{7}=\frac{*}{7}$

2 $3\frac{3}{5}=\frac{*}{5}$ **5** $3\frac{7}{8}=\frac{*}{8}$ **8** $1\frac{5}{12}=\frac{*}{12}$

3 $1\frac{7}{8}=\frac{*}{8}$ **6** $1\frac{8}{9}=\frac{*}{9}$ **9** $6\frac{3}{4}=\frac{*}{4}$

If you divide the numerator and the denominator of a fraction by the same number, the value of the fraction stays the same:

$\frac{15}{20}$ 5 is a factor of 15 and 20 so you can *divide numerator and denominator by 5:*

$\frac{15 \div 5}{20 \div 5} = \frac{3}{4}$ $\frac{15}{20}$ *is the same as* $\frac{3}{4}$

A fraction that is written with the **smallest possible numerator and denominator** is in its **lowest terms**.

$\frac{8 \div 4}{48 \div 4} = \frac{2 \div 2}{12 \div 2} = \frac{1}{6}$

$\frac{8}{48}$ in its **lowest terms** is $\frac{1}{6}$

Write the answer to $\frac{3}{4} + \frac{1}{12} = $ ✱ as a fraction in its **lowest terms**:

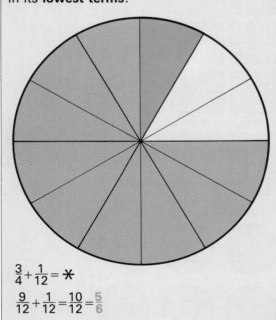

$\frac{3}{4} + \frac{1}{12} = $ ✱

$\frac{9}{12} + \frac{1}{12} = \frac{10}{12} = \frac{5}{6}$

A Copy and complete:

☆ $\frac{3}{15} = \frac{✱}{5}$ $\frac{3}{15} = \frac{1}{5}$

1 $\frac{6}{12} = \frac{✱}{4}$ 5 $\frac{12}{24} = \frac{✱}{8}$ 9 $\frac{9}{12} = \frac{3}{✱}$

2 $\frac{5}{15} = \frac{✱}{3}$ 6 $\frac{12}{18} = \frac{6}{✱}$ 10 $\frac{5}{20} = \frac{✱}{4}$

3 $\frac{10}{16} = \frac{5}{✱}$ 7 $\frac{6}{9} = \frac{✱}{3}$ 11 $\frac{7}{21} = \frac{1}{✱}$

4 $\frac{3}{9} = \frac{1}{✱}$ 8 $\frac{4}{10} = \frac{✱}{5}$ 12 $\frac{9}{18} = \frac{1}{✱}$

B Rewrite each fraction in its **lowest terms**:

☆ $\frac{6}{18}$ $\frac{1}{3}$

1 $\frac{12}{24}$ 5 $\frac{20}{25}$ 9 $\frac{9}{12}$

2 $\frac{16}{20}$ 6 $\frac{18}{24}$ 10 $\frac{24}{30}$

3 $\frac{18}{30}$ 7 $\frac{25}{30}$ 11 $\frac{10}{60}$

4 $\frac{14}{16}$ 8 $\frac{8}{12}$ 12 $\frac{16}{24}$

C Write each answer as a fraction in its **lowest terms**:

☆ $\frac{1}{2} - \frac{3}{10} = $ ✱ $\frac{5}{10} - \frac{3}{10} = \frac{2}{10} = \frac{1}{5}$

1 $\frac{1}{5} + \frac{2}{15} = $ ✱   4 $\frac{3}{4} - \frac{1}{20} = $ ✱

2 $\frac{1}{20} + \frac{3}{4} = $ ✱   5 $\frac{3}{4} - \frac{1}{5} = $ ✱

3 $\frac{1}{5} + \frac{3}{10} = $ ✱   6 $\frac{1}{4} - \frac{3}{20} = $ ✱

D Write these answers as **mixed numbers** with the fractions in **lowest terms**:

☆ $\frac{2}{3} + \frac{5}{6} = $ ✱ $\frac{4}{6} + \frac{5}{6} = \frac{9}{6} = 1\frac{3}{6} = 1\frac{1}{2}$

1 $\frac{5}{6} + \frac{1}{3} = $ ✱   4 $\frac{8}{9} + \frac{5}{18} = $ ✱

2 $\frac{3}{4} + \frac{5}{12} = $ ✱   5 $\frac{4}{5} + \frac{7}{10} = $ ✱

3 $\frac{19}{20} + \frac{3}{10} = $ ✱   6 $\frac{3}{4} + \frac{5}{6} = $ ✱

Fractions

To add fractions:
first rewrite them with the same denominator:

$$\frac{3}{8} + \frac{1}{4} = \frac{3}{8} + \frac{2}{8} = \frac{5}{8}$$

$$\frac{1}{3} + \frac{5}{6} = \frac{2}{6} + \frac{5}{6} = \frac{7}{6}$$

This can be written as a mixed number:

$$\frac{1}{3} + \frac{5}{6} = 1\frac{1}{6}$$

A Add these fractions:

☆ $\frac{3}{8} + \frac{1}{4} = $ ✱ $\frac{3}{8} + \frac{2}{8} = \frac{5}{8}$

1 $\frac{1}{3} + \frac{1}{6} = $ ✱   7 $\frac{3}{8} + \frac{1}{2} = $ ✱

2 $\frac{1}{2} + \frac{1}{8} = $ ✱   8 $\frac{3}{4} + \frac{1}{8} = $ ✱

3 $\frac{3}{5} + \frac{1}{10} = $ ✱   9 $\frac{1}{6} + \frac{1}{2} = $ ✱

4 $\frac{5}{8} + \frac{1}{4} = $ ✱   10 $\frac{5}{12} + \frac{1}{3} = $ ✱

5 $\frac{7}{10} + \frac{1}{5} = $ ✱   11 $\frac{2}{9} + \frac{1}{3} = $ ✱

6 $\frac{5}{6} + \frac{1}{12} = $ ✱   12 $\frac{1}{12} + \frac{3}{4} = $ ✱

B Add these fractions. Give your answer as a mixed number:

☆ $\frac{3}{5} + \frac{7}{10} = $ ✱ $\frac{6}{10} + \frac{7}{10} = \frac{13}{10} = 1\frac{3}{10}$

1 $\frac{3}{4} + \frac{5}{8} = $ ✱   4 $\frac{1}{2} + \frac{7}{8} = $ ✱

2 $\frac{9}{10} + \frac{1}{5} = $ ✱   5 $\frac{4}{5} + \frac{3}{10} = $ ✱

3 $\frac{5}{6} + \frac{2}{3} = $ ✱   6 $\frac{7}{12} + \frac{2}{3} = $ ✱

Two bags weigh $2\frac{1}{2}$ kg and $3\frac{1}{5}$ kg.
What is the total weight of the 2 two bags?

$$2\frac{1}{2} + 3\frac{1}{5} = ✱$$

*first write the fractions
with the same denominator*: $2\frac{5}{10} + 3\frac{2}{10} = ✱$

add the whole numbers: $2 + 3 = 5$

add the fractions: $\frac{5}{10} + \frac{2}{10} = \frac{7}{10}$

So: $2\frac{1}{2} + 3\frac{1}{5} = 5\frac{7}{10}$

The total weight of the 2 bags is $5\frac{7}{10}$ **kg.**

C Answer these questions:

☆ Joey walks $1\frac{1}{4}$ km in the morning and $2\frac{1}{5}$ km in the afternoon. How far does he walk altogether?

$1 + 2 = 3$
$\frac{5}{20} + \frac{4}{20} = \frac{9}{20}$
$3\frac{9}{20}$ km

1 In 2 races, a snail crawls $6\frac{1}{2}$ cm and $3\frac{1}{5}$ cm. How far does it crawl altogether?

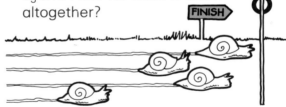

2 Two tables have lengths of $1\frac{3}{10}$ m and $1\frac{1}{4}$ m. How far do they stretch when placed end to end?

3 In a relay race, Jess runs $3\frac{1}{5}$ laps and Tom runs $4\frac{4}{10}$ laps. How many laps do they run altogether?

D Work out answers for these:

☆ $2\frac{1}{2} + 5\frac{1}{3} = $ ✱
$2 + 5 = 7$
$\frac{3}{6} + \frac{2}{6} = \frac{5}{6}$
$7 + \frac{5}{6} = 7\frac{5}{6}$

1 $2\frac{1}{3} + 1\frac{1}{4} = $ ✱   5 $3\frac{3}{5} + 1\frac{1}{4} = $ ✱

2 $3\frac{1}{5} + 2\frac{1}{4} = $ ✱   6 $6\frac{3}{4} + 4\frac{1}{10} = $ ✱

3 $3\frac{3}{10} + 1\frac{1}{4} = $ ✱   7 $4\frac{1}{6} + 1\frac{3}{4} = $ ✱

4 $2\frac{2}{5} + 1\frac{1}{3} = $ ✱   8 $2\frac{1}{4} + 5\frac{2}{5} = $ ✱

To subtract fractions:
first rewrite them with the same denominator:

$$\frac{5}{6} - \frac{1}{3} = \frac{5}{6} - \frac{2}{6} = \frac{3}{6}$$

What is the difference in length between these two lines?

—————————— $(3\frac{1}{5}$ cm)

————————————$(5\frac{9}{10}$ cm)

$$5\frac{9}{10} - 3\frac{1}{5} = \text{✱}$$

$$5\frac{9}{10} - 3\frac{2}{10} = \text{✱}$$

subtract the whole numbers: $5 - 3 = 2$

subtract the fractions: $\frac{9}{10} - \frac{2}{10} = \frac{7}{10}$

So: $5\frac{9}{10} - 3\frac{2}{10} = 2\frac{7}{10}$

The difference in length is $2\frac{7}{10}$ cm.

In a pie eating contest, Podgy ate $8\frac{1}{4}$ pies and Porky ate $5\frac{2}{3}$ pies. How many more pies did Podgy eat than Porky?

$$8\frac{1}{4} - 5\frac{2}{3} = \text{✱}$$
$$8\frac{3}{12} - 5\frac{8}{12} = \text{✱}$$

You cannot subtract $\frac{8}{12}$ from $\frac{3}{12}$. So:
rewrite $8\frac{3}{12}$ as $7\frac{15}{12}$: $7\frac{15}{12} - 5\frac{8}{12} = \text{✱}$

subtract the whole numbers: $7 - 5 = 2$

subtract the fractions: $\frac{15}{12} - \frac{8}{12} = \frac{7}{12}$

So: $8\frac{1}{4} - 5\frac{2}{3} = 2\frac{7}{12}$

Podgy ate $2\frac{7}{12}$ more pies than Porky.

A Subtract these fractions:

☆ $\frac{5}{8} - \frac{1}{2} = \text{✱}$ $\frac{5}{8} - \frac{4}{8} = \frac{1}{8}$

1 $\frac{3}{8} - \frac{1}{4} = \text{✱}$ 5 $\frac{3}{4} - \frac{3}{8} = \text{✱}$

2 $\frac{5}{6} - \frac{2}{3} = \text{✱}$ 6 $\frac{5}{6} - \frac{7}{12} = \text{✱}$

3 $\frac{7}{8} - \frac{1}{2} = \text{✱}$ 7 $\frac{7}{8} - \frac{3}{4} = \text{✱}$

4 $\frac{1}{2} - \frac{1}{8} = \text{✱}$ 8 $\frac{9}{10} - \frac{3}{5} = \text{✱}$

B Work out the **difference** in length between each pair of lines:

☆ ——————————————— $(4\frac{2}{5}$ cm)

————————— $(2\frac{1}{10}$ cm) $4\frac{4}{10}$ cm $- 2\frac{1}{10}$ cm $= 2\frac{3}{10}$ cm

1 ——————————————————— $(5\frac{3}{10}$ cm)

——————————————— $(4\frac{1}{5}$ cm)

2 ———————————————— $(5\frac{7}{10}$ cm)

—————————————————— $(7\frac{9}{10}$ cm)

3 ———— $(1\frac{1}{2}$ cm)

—————————————— $(6\frac{7}{10}$ cm)

4 ————— $(2\frac{1}{2}$ cm)

——————————————— $(6\frac{9}{10}$ cm)

C What is the **difference** between:

☆ $6\frac{1}{4}$ days and $3\frac{5}{8}$ days? $6\frac{2}{8} - 3\frac{5}{8} = \text{✱}$
$5\frac{10}{8} - 3\frac{5}{8} = 2\frac{5}{8}$

1 $7\frac{1}{2}$ hours and $3\frac{3}{4}$ hours? $2\frac{5}{8}$ days

2 $5\frac{1}{2}$ kg and $2\frac{7}{10}$ kg?

3 $3\frac{1}{8}$ days and $2\frac{3}{4}$ days?

4 $4\frac{1}{5}$ metres and $1\frac{1}{4}$ metres?

5 $4\frac{2}{3}$ hours and $1\frac{3}{4}$ hours?

6 $3\frac{1}{4}$ hours and $2\frac{5}{6}$ hours?

7 $6\frac{2}{5}$ metres and $3\frac{1}{2}$ metres?

8 $7\frac{1}{10}$ kg and $2\frac{3}{4}$ kg?

D Work out the answers to these:

☆ $5\frac{1}{3} - 1\frac{3}{4} = \text{✱}$ $5\frac{4}{12} - 1\frac{9}{12} = \text{✱}$
$4\frac{16}{12} - 1\frac{9}{12} = 3\frac{7}{12}$

1 $6\frac{1}{5} - 1\frac{9}{10} = \text{✱}$ 6 $6\frac{1}{10} - 2\frac{3}{4} = \text{✱}$

2 $9\frac{2}{5} - 4\frac{3}{4} = \text{✱}$ 7 $6\frac{1}{2} - 3\frac{2}{3} = \text{✱}$

3 $7\frac{1}{6} - 2\frac{1}{4} = \text{✱}$ 8 $6\frac{1}{4} - 3\frac{2}{3} = \text{✱}$

4 $3\frac{1}{3} - 1\frac{3}{4} = \text{✱}$ 9 $5\frac{3}{10} - 2\frac{3}{4} = \text{✱}$

5 $7\frac{3}{5} - 1\frac{2}{3} = \text{✱}$ 10 $4\frac{1}{5} - 2\frac{1}{4} = \text{✱}$

Percentages

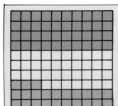

There are **100** small squares in this diagram.

40 out of **100** squares are blue.

Say: '**40 per cent** of the squares are blue'
Write: **40%** of the squares are blue.
40% means **40 out of 100** or $\frac{40}{100}$.

23 out of 100 squares are grey.
23% of the squares are grey.

A What **percentage** of each diagram below is shaded?

☆ 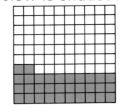   **32%**

1 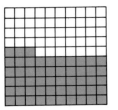   5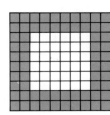

2 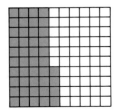   6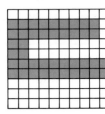

3 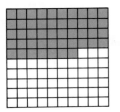   7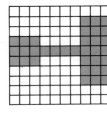

4 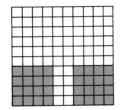   8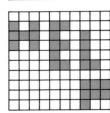

B Write as a **percentage**:

☆ 32 out of 100   **32%**

1 27 out of 100   6 80 out of 100

2 15 out of 100   7 5 out of 100

3 30 out of 100   8 99 out of 100

4 62 out of 100   9 11 out of 100

5 67 out of 100   10 2 out of 100

C Write as a **percentage**:

☆ $\frac{63}{100}$ **63%**

1 $\frac{36}{100}$ 6 $\frac{47}{100}$

2 $\frac{54}{100}$ 7 $\frac{86}{100}$

3 $\frac{31}{100}$ 8 $\frac{9}{100}$

4 $\frac{50}{100}$ 9 $\frac{7}{100}$

5 $\frac{17}{100}$ 10 $\frac{50}{100}$

D Copy and complete:

☆ $\frac{7}{10}=\frac{*}{100}= *\%$ $\frac{7}{10}=\frac{70}{100}=70\%$

1 $\frac{5}{10}=\frac{*}{100}= *\%$

2 $\frac{9}{10}=\frac{*}{100}= *\%$

3 $\frac{1}{10}=\frac{*}{100}= *\%$

4 $\frac{2}{5}=\frac{*}{10}=\frac{*}{100}= *\%$

5 $\frac{4}{5}=\frac{*}{10}=\frac{*}{100}= *\%$

6 $\frac{1}{2}=\frac{*}{10}=\frac{*}{100}= *\%$

7 $\frac{1}{20}=\frac{*}{100}= *\%$

8 $\frac{3}{5}=\frac{*}{10}=\frac{*}{100}= *\%$

9 $\frac{3}{10}=\frac{*}{100}= *\%$

10 $\frac{3}{20}=\frac{*}{100}= *\%$

A Write each of these percentages as a fraction in its **lowest terms**:

☆ 15% $15\% = \frac{15}{100} = \frac{3}{20}$

1 20%   4 90%   7 5%
2 40%   5 10%   8 55%
3 60%   6 80%   9 35%

$\frac{1}{4}$ of this diagram is shaded.

25 out of 100 squares are shaded.

25% of the squares are shaded.

$\frac{1}{4}$=**25%**

$\frac{3}{4}$ of the diagram is not shaded.
75% of the squares are not shaded.
$\frac{3}{4}$=**75%**

B Write as **percentages**:

☆ $\frac{1}{5}$ $\frac{1}{5} = \frac{2}{10} = \frac{20}{100} = 20\%$

1 $\frac{1}{10}$ 4 $\frac{6}{10}$ 7 $\frac{2}{5}$
2 $\frac{3}{10}$ 5 $\frac{7}{10}$ 8 1 whole
3 $\frac{8}{10}$ 6 $\frac{3}{5}$ 9 $\frac{4}{5}$

D

EVERYTHING MUST GO!

How much money will you save on each item?

C **Answer these questions:**

☆ In a darts competition, the prize money is £20. If Bill wins 20% of the money, how much does he win?

$20\% = \frac{20}{100} = \frac{2}{10} = \frac{1}{5}$
$\frac{1}{5}$ of £20 = £4

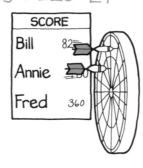

SCORE
Bill   82
Annie
Fred   360

☆

chair £30
sale offer
10% off

$10\% = \frac{10}{100} = \frac{1}{10}$
$\frac{1}{10}$ of £30 = £3
total saving £3

4 spin drier
£120
sale offer
25% off

1
tea set
£40
sale offer
10% off

2 typewriter £80
sale offer 25% off

5 camera
£90
sale offer
30% off

1 Annie is given 10% of £30. How much money does she receive?

2 Fred wins 50% of £40. How much does he win?

3 In a sale, 20% is taken off every item. How much do you save if you buy a vase costing £40?

4 Mrs Jay has £120. She spends 30% of this money on a coat. What is the cost of the coat?

3

fridge £160
sale offer 20% off

6 train set £20
special sale offer
75% off

A Copy and complete:

1   $3 = \frac{*}{5}$ 6 $\frac{12}{3} = *$

2   $2 = \frac{*}{10}$ 7 $\frac{20}{4} = *$

3   $4 = \frac{*}{2}$ 8 $\frac{30}{5} = *$

4   $5 = \frac{*}{3}$ 9 $\frac{32}{8} = *$

5   $3 = \frac{*}{8}$ 10 $\frac{24}{4} = *$

B Copy and complete:

1   $2\frac{2}{3} = \frac{*}{3}$ 6 $2\frac{3}{8} = \frac{*}{8}$

2   $1\frac{5}{8} = \frac{*}{8}$ 7 $4\frac{1}{4} = \frac{*}{4}$

3   $3\frac{1}{4} = \frac{*}{4}$ 8 $7\frac{1}{2} = \frac{*}{2}$

4   $1\frac{5}{6} = \frac{*}{6}$ 9 $6\frac{1}{5} = \frac{*}{5}$

5   $4\frac{3}{5} = \frac{*}{5}$ 10 $7\frac{3}{4} = \frac{*}{4}$

C Rewrite each pair of fractions so that they have the same **denominator**:

1   $\frac{1}{2}$ and $\frac{1}{4}$ 6 $\frac{1}{3}$ and $\frac{3}{4}$

2   $\frac{1}{3}$ and $\frac{1}{2}$ 7 $\frac{1}{5}$ and $\frac{1}{4}$

3   $\frac{1}{5}$ and $\frac{3}{10}$ 8 $\frac{1}{10}$ and $\frac{3}{4}$

4   $\frac{1}{2}$ and $\frac{7}{10}$ 9 $\frac{2}{5}$ and $\frac{2}{3}$

5   $\frac{1}{4}$ and $\frac{1}{3}$ 10 $\frac{9}{10}$ and $\frac{3}{4}$

D Add these fractions:

1   $\frac{1}{4} + \frac{3}{8} = *$ 6 $2\frac{1}{4} + 1\frac{1}{2} = *$

2   $\frac{3}{10} + \frac{2}{5} = *$ 7 $3\frac{1}{3} + 4\frac{1}{2} = *$

3   $\frac{1}{6} + \frac{2}{3} = *$ 8 $1\frac{1}{5} + 3\frac{2}{3} = *$

4   $\frac{1}{2} + \frac{2}{3} = *$ 9 $2\frac{3}{4} + 3\frac{2}{5} = *$

5   $\frac{3}{5} + \frac{1}{2} = *$ 10 $4\frac{3}{4} + 3\frac{2}{3} = *$

E Subtract these fractions:

1   $\frac{7}{8} - \frac{1}{4} = *$ 5 $4\frac{4}{5} - 2\frac{3}{10} = *$

2   $\frac{5}{6} - \frac{1}{3} = *$ 6 $5\frac{1}{3} - 2\frac{5}{6} = *$

3   $\frac{3}{4} - \frac{3}{8} = *$ 7 $6\frac{1}{2} - 2\frac{2}{3} = *$

4   $3\frac{7}{10} - 1\frac{1}{5} = *$ 8 $4\frac{1}{3} - 1\frac{3}{4} = *$

F Rewrite each fraction in its **lowest terms**:

1   $\frac{5}{10}$ 4 $\frac{4}{20}$ 7 $\frac{12}{16}$

2   $\frac{8}{12}$ 5 $\frac{8}{10}$ 8 $\frac{10}{15}$

3   $\frac{6}{9}$ 6 $\frac{9}{12}$ 9 $\frac{6}{21}$

G What **percentage** of each diagram is shaded?

1
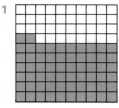

3
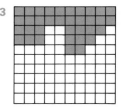

2
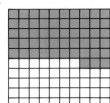

4
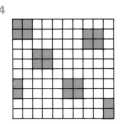

H Copy and complete this table:

	fraction	percentage
1		10%
2	$\frac{7}{10}$	
3	$\frac{1}{5}$	
4		30%
5		60%
6	$\frac{8}{10}$	

For each fraction below, find a balloon with the same value.
Write down the letter tied to the balloon.
What is the hidden message?

Example: $\frac{1}{5}$=20% so write M

Word 1 $\frac{1}{5}$ $\frac{3}{10}$ $\frac{4}{5}$ $\frac{8}{10}$ $\frac{35}{100}$

Word 2 $\frac{1}{4}$ $\frac{3}{5}$ $\frac{3}{10}$ $\frac{98}{100}$ $\frac{2}{5}$ $\frac{3}{5}$ $\frac{1}{4}$

Word 3 $\frac{25}{100}$ $\frac{60}{100}$ $\frac{3}{4}$ $\frac{1}{4}$

Word 4 $\frac{75}{100}$ $\frac{5}{5}$

Word 5 $\frac{1}{10}$ $\frac{70}{100}$ $\frac{2}{5}$ $\frac{6}{10}$ $\frac{25}{100}$

Word 6 $\frac{1}{2}$ $\frac{7}{10}$ $\frac{9}{20}$ $\frac{1}{10}$ $\frac{45}{100}$

Word 7 $\frac{1}{2}$ $\frac{6}{10}$ $\frac{3}{4}$ $\frac{3}{20}$ $\frac{1}{10}$

Word 8 $\frac{9}{10}$ $\frac{3}{4}$ $\frac{50}{100}$

Word 9 $\frac{11}{20}$ $\frac{3}{4}$ $\frac{4}{5}$ $\frac{8}{10}$ $\frac{1}{10}$ $\frac{45}{100}$

Word 10 $\frac{75}{100}$ $\frac{100}{100}$

Word 11 $\frac{6}{20}$ $\frac{64}{100}$ $\frac{3}{10}$

Word 12 $\frac{4}{10}$ $\frac{98}{100}$ $\frac{4}{4}$

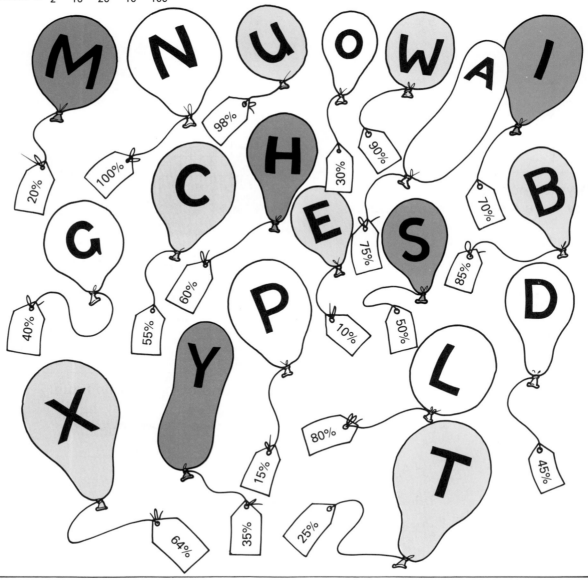

A You need: centimetre squared paper.

Design a garden that covers 100 squares on your centimetre squared paper.

Your garden should have areas for vegetables, flowers, shrubs, grass, a patio and a path.

Each area should cover a whole number of squares.

Write down the percentage of the whole garden that you have allowed for each area.

B Imagine that you are in charge of a class of young children who have never heard of fractions before. Suddenly, one boy brings you this piece of paper. The boy says that he has found these strange signs written in a book and he wants to know what they mean.

$$\frac{1}{2} \qquad 5\frac{3}{4} \qquad \frac{20}{10} \qquad \frac{12}{5}$$

Write in your own words how you would explain the 'strange signs' to the boy. You can also use any diagrams and equipment that may be helpful.

Design an enjoyable activity that would help the child to understand fractions.

C Find out the answers to these questions:

To the nearest second, how long does it take you to walk 100 m?

At this pace how long would it take you to walk:
a) 1 km?   b) 10 km?   c) 100 km?   d) 1000 km?

What is the distance from the Earth to the Moon in kilometres?

How old are you on your next birthday?

Use the information above to solve this problem:

There is a road from the Earth to the Moon and you will start walking along this road on your next birthday. If you are able to walk without stopping at the same pace that you walked for 100 m, how old will you be when you reach the moon?

Answer any questions you can. Leave those you cannot do.

Write the correct time for these clocks:

1 18 minutes slow

2 35 minutes fast

Write these times as 24-hour clock times:

3 7.30 am   5 12.16 pm

4 2.25 pm   6 12.23 am

Write these times as am or pm times:

7 09.34   10 23.56

8 13.52   11 00.03

9 08.08   12 21.42

	train 1	train 2
Hanby	07.15	08.55
Burston	07.43	09.22
Ulpool	08.01	09.40
Pinhook	09.09	10.54

13 How long does Train 1 take to complete the whole journey?

14 How long does Train 2 take to travel from Burston to Pinhook?

15 Which train takes longer to travel from Hanby to Ulpool?

16 Which train would you catch if you had to be in Ulpool at 9.30 a m?

Choose the correct answer for each of these questions:

17 In 1 second an athlete could run:
    a) 10 m   b) 20 m   c) 50 m

18 In 10 seconds your pulse could beat: a) 3 times   b) 11 times
    c) 30 times

Rewrite these pairs of fractions so that they both have the same denominator:

19 $\frac{3}{4}$ $\frac{5}{8}$ 21 $\frac{5}{6}$ $\frac{5}{9}$

20 $\frac{1}{3}$ $\frac{2}{5}$

Write these improper fractions as whole numbers:

(22) $\frac{12}{4}$ (23) $\frac{32}{8}$

Write these mixed numbers as improper fractions:

(24) $4\frac{7}{8}$ (25) $6\frac{7}{10}$

Answer these and write the fraction in lowest terms:

(26) $\frac{2}{3} + \frac{7}{12} = $ ✱

(27) $\frac{3}{4} - \frac{3}{20} = $ ✱

(28) $4\frac{4}{5} + 2\frac{7}{10} = $ ✱

(29) $10\frac{1}{3} - 2\frac{5}{6} = $ ✱

Write as a percentage:

30 35 out of 100   33 $\frac{6}{100}$

31 16 out of 100   34 $\frac{3}{10}$

32 $\frac{72}{100}$ (35) $\frac{17}{20}$

Write each of these percentages as a fraction in lowest terms:

(36) 40%

(37) 35%

(38) 75%

39 How much do you save on a computer costing £90 when the cost is reduced by 30%?

(40) 35% of the children in a school can swim 10 metres. If there are 140 children in the school, how many cannot swim 10 m?

Area

A What is the **area** of each shape below?

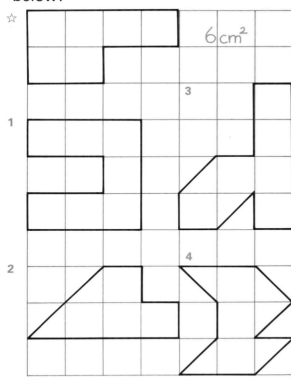

6 cm²

B You need some centimetre squared paper.

☆ Draw a square that has an area of 4 cm².

1 Draw a square that has an area of 16 cm².

2 Draw a rectangle that has an area of 27 cm².

3 Draw a right angled triangle that has an area of 8 cm².

C Find the **approximate area** of this shape:

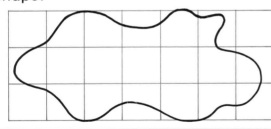

D Use **multiplication** to work out the areas of these gardens:

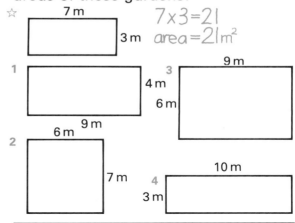

7 × 3 = 21
area = 21 m²

E Work out the area of each **blue** triangle:

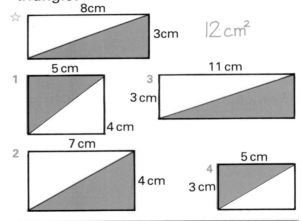

12 cm²

F Work out these floor areas:

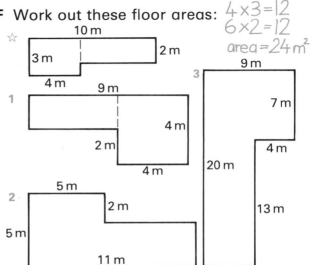

4 × 3 = 12
6 × 2 = 12
area = 24 m²

To find the area of this shape,
first divide it into triangles and rectangles:

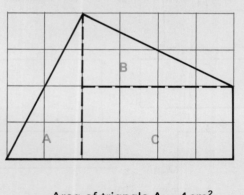

Area of triangle A= 4 cm²
Area of triangle B= 4 cm²
Area of rectangle C= 8 cm²
Total area of the shape= **16 cm²**

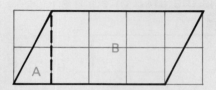

If you cut a triangle from the side of a
parallelogram, you can re-arrange the
two pieces to form a rectangle.

**The parallelogram and the rectangle have
the same area.**

A 1 Copy the shapes below on centimetre
squared paper.

2 Divide each shape into triangles and
rectangles.

3 Work out the area of each shape.

B 1 Draw the parallelograms below on
centimetre squared paper.

2 Change each parallelogram to a
rectangle with the same area.

3 Write the area of each shape.

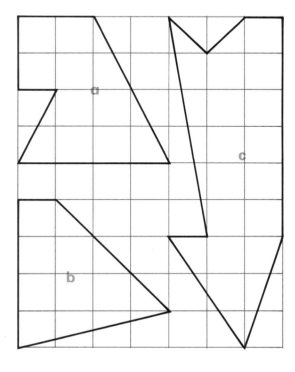

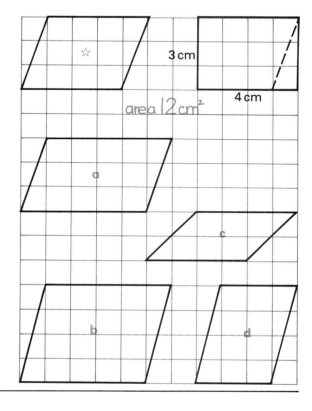

3 cm

4 cm

area 12 cm²

Area

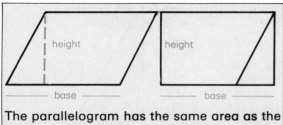

The parallelogram has the same area as the rectangle:

$$\text{area of rectangle} = \textbf{base} \times \textbf{height}$$
$3 \times 2 = 6$; so area of rectangle = **6cm²**
$$\text{area of parallelogram} = \textbf{base} \times \textbf{height}$$
$3 \times 2 = 6$; so area of parallelogram = **6cm²**

A For each parallelogram below, measure the **base** and the **height** and work out the **area**:

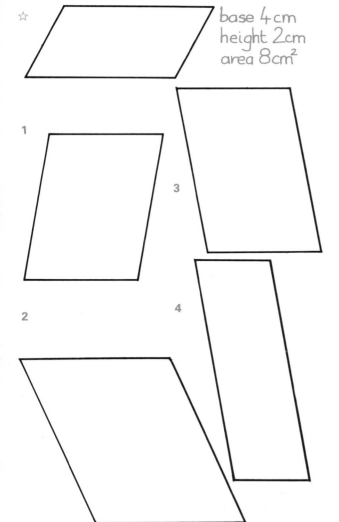

☆ base 4 cm
height 2 cm
area 8 cm²

1

2

3

4

B

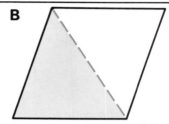

1 What is the area of this parallelogram?

2 What is the name of the blue line?

3 What fraction of the parallelogram is shaded?

4 What is the area of the shaded section?

C Work out the **area** of each parallelogram and the **area** of each shaded triangle:

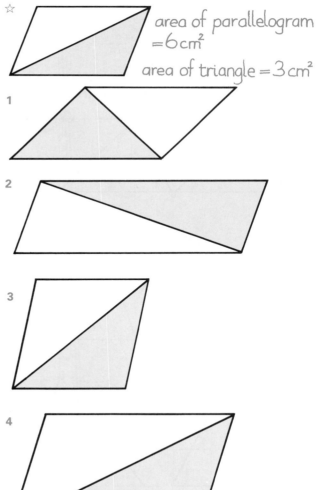

☆ area of parallelogram
= 6 cm²

area of triangle = 3 cm²

1

2

3

4

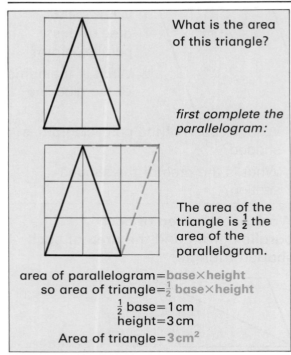

What is the area of this triangle?

first complete the parallelogram:

The area of the triangle is $\frac{1}{2}$ the area of the parallelogram.

area of parallelogram=**base×height**
so area of triangle=$\frac{1}{2}$ **base×height**
$\frac{1}{2}$ base=1cm
height=3cm
Area of triangle=**3cm²**

A Work out the **area** of each triangle:

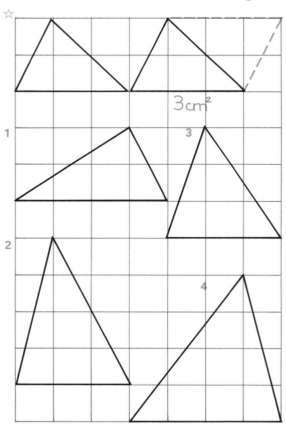

3cm²

1

2

3

4

B Work out the area of each sail:

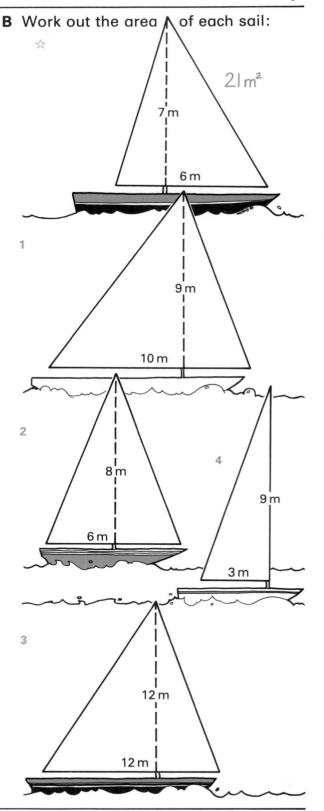

21m²

7 m

6 m

1

9 m

10 m

2

8 m

6 m

4

9 m

3 m

3

12 m

12 m

A How many children can fit onto a netball court?

It will help you to find out first how many children can stand in a square metre without leaning outwards.

Can all the children in your school fit into one netball court?

If they can, what area of space will be left free when all the children are standing on the court?

B Jody has drawn 4 circles on centimetre squared paper.

The circles have the same centre.

The radii of the circles are 1 cm, 2 cm, 3 cm and 4 cm.

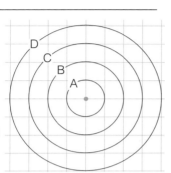

She says that the area of circle B is about 4 times the area of circle A and that the area of circle C is about 9 times the area of circle A. She has not been able to work out how many times greater than the area of circle A is circle D.

Draw a diagram on centimetre squared paper. Do you agree with Jody's answers so far?

Can you help her with the question she cannot answer?

C Here is the plan of part of a house.

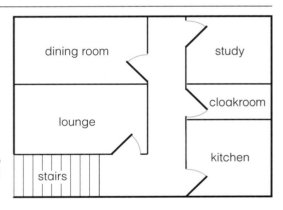

On centimetre squared paper draw a plan for the upstairs and the downstairs of a house. Each square on your paper should represent 1 m² of space. The total area of each floor should measure 12 m by 8 m.

Your house must include cupboards, toilets, a kitchen and all of the other rooms you will need. Don't forget to leave space for the stairs on each floor.

When you have finished your plan, work out the approximate floor area of each room.

Answer any questions you can. Leave those you cannot do.

These shapes have been drawn on centimetre squared paper.

What is the area of each shape?

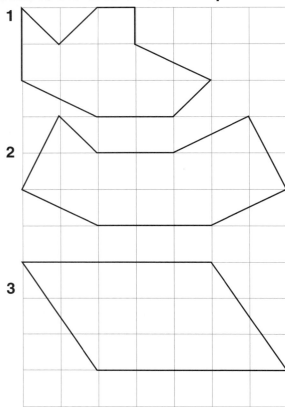

1

2

3

Work out these floor areas in square metres:

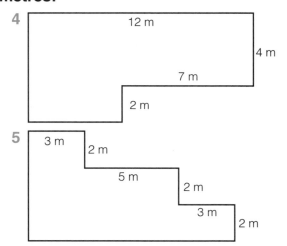

4

12 m

4 m

7 m

2 m

5

3 m

2 m

5 m

2 m

3 m

2 m

Work out the areas of these parallelograms:

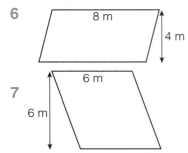

6

8 m

4 m

7

6 m

6 m

Work out the areas of these triangles:

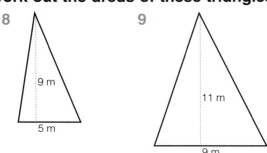

8

9 m

5 m

9

11 m

9 m

Use a calculator to work out the length of this carpet:

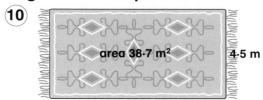

(10)

area 38·7 m²

4·5 m

If carpet costs £5.50 per square metre, what would be the cost of carpeting this corridor?

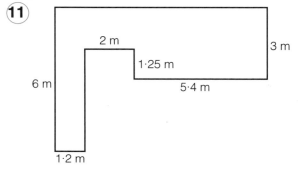

(11)

2 m

3 m

1·25 m

6 m

5·4 m

1·2 m

Volume

A The layers below have been made with centimetre cubes.
Work out the **volume** of each layer:

☆ 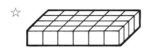 24 cm³

1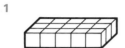

4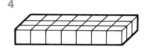

2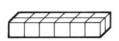

5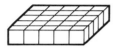

3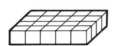

6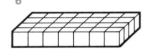

B The cuboids below have been made with centimetre cubes.
Work out the **volume** of each cuboid:

☆ 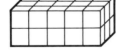 30 cm³

1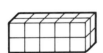

4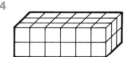

2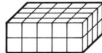

5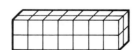

3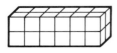

6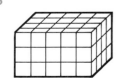

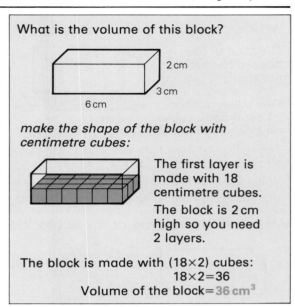

What is the volume of this block?

2 cm
3 cm
6 cm

make the shape of the block with centimetre cubes:

The first layer is made with 18 centimetre cubes.

The block is 2 cm high so you need 2 layers.

The block is made with (18×2) cubes:
18×2=36
Volume of the block=**36 cm³**

C Work out the **volume** of each block:

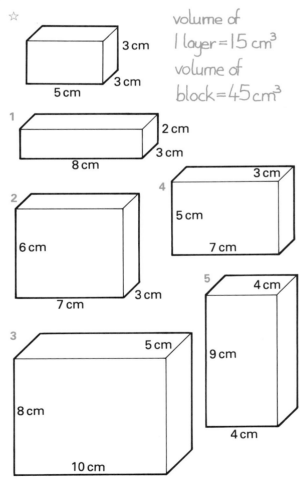

☆ 3 cm
3 cm
5 cm

volume of
1 layer = 15 cm³
volume of
block = 45 cm³

1   2 cm   3 cm   8 cm

2   6 cm   7 cm   3 cm

4   3 cm   5 cm   7 cm

3   5 cm   8 cm   10 cm

5   4 cm   9 cm   4 cm

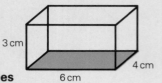

What is the volume of this block?

The area of the base of the block is **24 cm²**:

This tells you that **24 centimetre cubes** make up the first layer.

The height of **3 cm** tells you that **3 layers** are needed.   24×3 =72

Volume of the block   =**72 cm³**

Volume of the block=**area of base×height**

3 cm, 6 cm, 4 cm

1 cubic centimetre has the same volume as 1 millilitre.

1 cm³=1 ml

This box can be filled with **100 centimetre cubes**.
The **capacity** of the box is **100 ml**.

4 cm, 5 cm, 5 cm

A Work out the **volume** of these blocks:

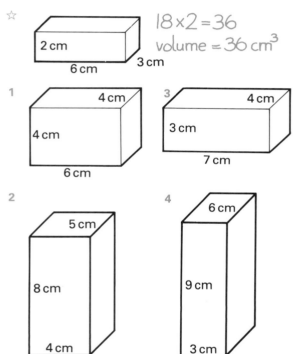

☆ 2 cm, 6 cm, 3 cm
18×2=36
volume =36 cm³

1   4 cm, 4 cm, 6 cm

3   4 cm, 3 cm, 7 cm

2   5 cm, 8 cm, 4 cm

4   6 cm, 9 cm, 3 cm

B Copy and complete:

cuboid	area of base	height	volume
☆	16 cm²	2 cm	32 cm³
1	22 cm²	3 cm	
2	40 cm²	6 cm	
3	35 cm²	4 cm	
4	20 cm²		60 cm³
5		5 cm	45 cm³

C Work out the **capacity** of each box:

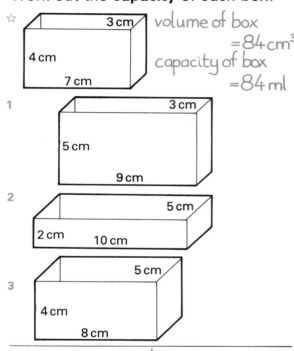

☆   3 cm, 4 cm, 7 cm
volume of box =84 cm³
capacity of box =84 ml

1   3 cm, 5 cm, 9 cm

2   5 cm, 2 cm, 10 cm

3   5 cm, 4 cm, 8 cm

D Which box below has a **capacity**:

1 of exactly 1 litre?

2 greater than 1 litre?

3 less than 1 litre?

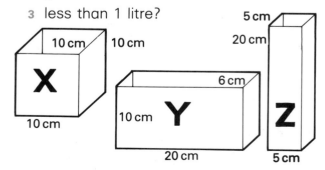

X   10 cm, 10 cm, 10 cm

Y   10 cm, 6 cm, 20 cm

Z   5 cm, 20 cm, 5 cm

Mixed Problems

A Carpet costs £5·25 per square metre. Work out the cost of carpet for these rooms and corridors:

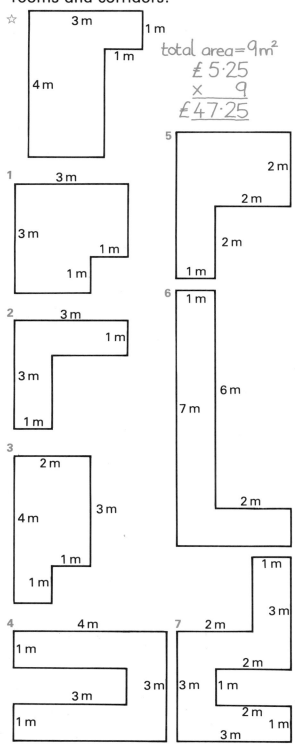

☆ total area=9m²
£ 5·25
× 9
£47·25

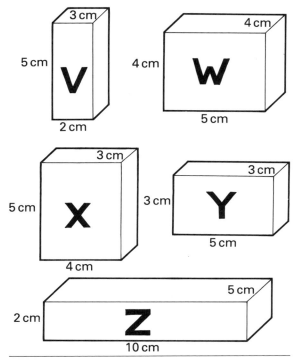

B Copy and complete this block graph to show the capacities of the containers above:

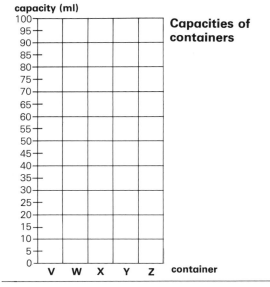

C If the containers are filled with a liquid costing 10p per millilitre, what is the cost of filling each container?

☆ Container **V** capacity=30 ml   £3

A Work out the **area** of each shape:

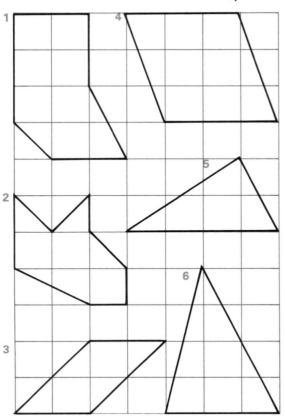

B Work out the **area** of each sail:

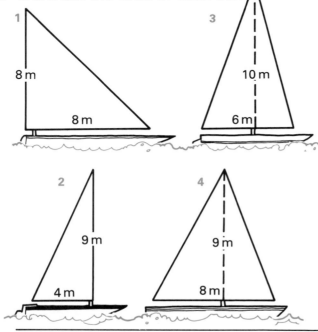

C Work out the **volume** of each block, **in cubic centimetres**:

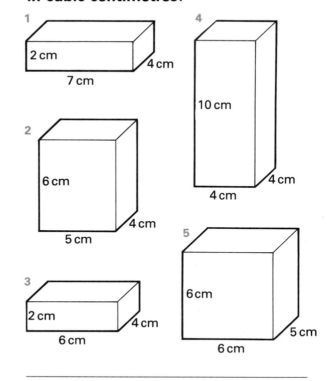

D Work out the **capacity** of each box, **in millilitres**:

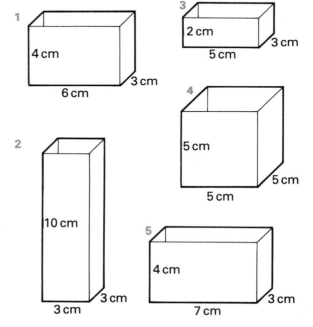

Decimals

A Show the shaded parts of these shapes as a **fraction** and as a **decimal**:

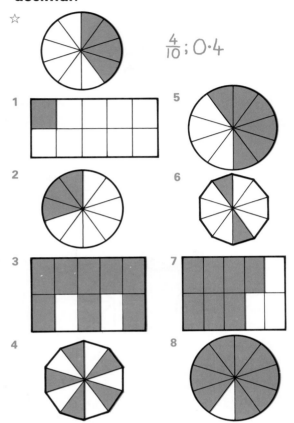

☆ $\frac{4}{10}$; 0·4

B Write these fractions as **decimals**:

☆ $\frac{27}{100}$ 0·27

1 $\frac{9}{10}$ 5 $\frac{83}{100}$

2 $\frac{24}{100}$ 6 $\frac{5}{10}$

3 $\frac{6}{10}$ 7 $\frac{49}{100}$

4 $\frac{17}{100}$ 8 $\frac{33}{100}$

C Write these decimals as **fractions**:

☆ 0·36 $\frac{36}{100}$

1 0·9   5 0·35

2 0·6   6 0·51

3 0·3   7 0·63

4 0·7   8 0·85

D Write the number shown on each abacus in 2 different ways:

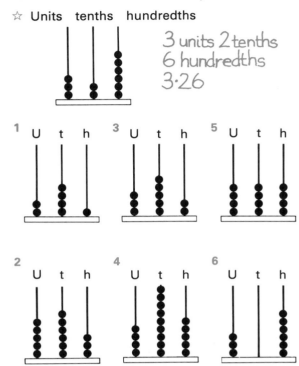

☆ Units   tenths   hundredths

3 units 2 tenths 6 hundredths
3·26

E Copy and complete:

☆ $\begin{array}{r} 1\,4·6\,8 \\ +\,1\,2·8\,5 \\ \hline \end{array}$ $\begin{array}{r} 1\,4·6\,8 \\ +\,1\,2·8\,5 \\ \hline 2\,7·5\,3 \end{array}$

1 $\begin{array}{r} 1\,2·9\,5 \\ +\,\ \ 6·2\,7 \\ \hline \end{array}$ 3 $\begin{array}{r} 9·3\,6 \\ +\,1\,2·7\,5 \\ \hline \end{array}$ 5 $\begin{array}{r} 2\,3·6\,2 \\ +\,1\,8·0\,9 \\ \hline \end{array}$

2 $\begin{array}{r} 1\,0·6\,3 \\ +\,\ \ 4·9\,2 \\ \hline \end{array}$ 4 $\begin{array}{r} 1\,6·0\,7 \\ +\,1\,9·9\,9 \\ \hline \end{array}$ 6 $\begin{array}{r} 4\,7·6\,6 \\ +\,6\,7·4\,4 \\ \hline \end{array}$

F Work out the **difference** between:

☆ 25·23 and 6·91

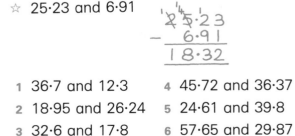

1 36·7 and 12·3   4 45·72 and 36·37

2 18·95 and 26·24   5 24·61 and 39·8

3 32·6 and 17·8   6 57·65 and 29·87

shape 1

shape 4

shape 2

shape 5

shape 3

shape 6

A Copy this table:

shape	estimate (cm)	measure (cm)	difference (cm)
1			
2			
3			
4			
5			
6			

B 1 Estimate the perimeter of each shape above to the nearest centimetre.

2 Write the estimates in your table.

3 Measure each perimeter to the nearest $\frac{1}{2}$ cm.

4 Write the measures in your table.

5 Work out the difference between each estimate and the measure.

6 Write the differences in the table.

C Answer these questions:

☆ A length of material is 2·86 m. How much material is left after 1·38 m has been cut off?

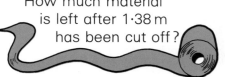

$$2 \cdot \overset{7}{8}\overset{1}{6}$$
$$\underline{1 \cdot 38}$$
$$1 \cdot 48 \text{m}$$

1 A rectangle has sides of 1·73 m and 1·85 m. What is the perimeter of the rectangle?

2 A piece of ribbon is 7·38 cm long. If it is cut into 3 equal pieces, what is the length of each piece?

3 5 square sections with sides of 3·49 m are used to make a tower. What is the height of the tower?

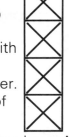

4 A race track is 4·65 km long. After Speedy has driven 2·98 km, how much further must he drive to complete the lap?

5 A bus driver makes 8 journeys of 17·65 km. How far does he drive altogether?

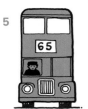

6 A rope is 23·12 m long. If it is cut into 8 equal pieces, what is the length of each piece?

7 A car is 1·62 m wide. A garage is 2·41 m wide. How much width is left when the car is in the garage?

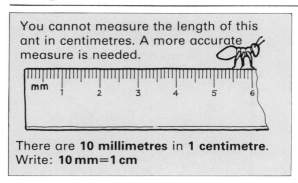

You cannot measure the length of this ant in centimetres. A more accurate measure is needed.

There are **10 millimetres** in **1 centimetre**. Write: **10 mm=1 cm**

10 mm=1 cm
1 mm=$\frac{1}{10}$ cm or **0·1 cm**

The length of this line is **6 cm 4 mm**. Write: **6.4 cm**

A How many **millimetres** in:

☆ 2 cm?   20

1 3 cm?   4 $\frac{1}{2}$ cm?   7 7 cm?

2 5 cm?   5 $1\frac{1}{2}$ cm?   8 10 cm?

3 4 cm?   6 9 cm?   9 20 cm?

B Measure these lines as accurately as you can. Give each answer in **centimetres** and **millimetres**:

☆ ————————   4 cm 3 mm

1 ————————

2 ————

3 —————————

4 ———————

5 ————————

C Measure these lines as accurately as you can. Give each answer in **millimetres**:

☆ ————————   52 mm

1 —————

2 ——————

3 ————————

4 —————————

5 —————————

D Write these lengths in **centimetres**:

☆ 82 mm   8·2 cm

1 3 cm 2 mm   6 95 mm

2 5 cm 6 mm   7 10 cm 4 mm

3 24 mm   8 101 mm

4 65 mm   9 96 mm

5 8 cm 3 mm   10 18 cm 4 mm

E Write these lengths in **centimetres** and **millimetres**:

☆ 3·6 cm   3 cm 6 mm

1 2·8 cm   7 5·1 cm

2 1·9 cm   8 0·6 cm

3 6·4 cm   9 3·2 cm

4 7·9 cm   10 0·9 cm

5 3·8 cm   11 11·6 cm

6 4·7 cm   12 24·3 cm

F Write these lengths, **to the nearest centimetre**:

☆ 8·5 cm   9 cm

1 3·2 cm   7 10·4 cm

2 5·8 cm   8 11·5 cm

3 9·6 cm   9 27·9 cm

4 4·4 cm   10 50·5 cm

5 16·7 cm   11 26·8 cm

6 24·2 cm   12 14·5 cm

A Measure these lengths as accurately as you can:

☆ the diameter of a 2 pence coin

2·6 cm

1 the perimeter of this square

2 the length of this screw

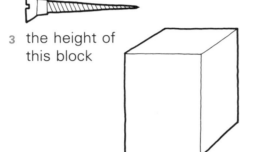

3 the height of this block

4 the length of this rod

5 the radius of this wheel

6 the length of this needle

7 this piece of elastic, unstretched and stretched

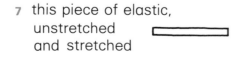

Super Spider has just started the 10 centimetre marathon.
So far he has dropped 63 mm.
How much further has he still to drop?

10 mm = **1 cm**
100 mm = 10 cm

100 mm − 63 mm = 37 mm

Super Spider still has 37 mm to drop.

B How much further have these spiders still to drop in the **10 cm marathon**?

Millie   14 mm

☆   1   2   3   4   5   6

Creepy   Winnie

Minnie   Weenie

Millie   Lizzie

Fuzzy

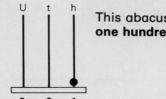

This abacus shows **one hundredth** ($\frac{1}{100}$)

0 · 0 1

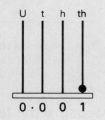

To divide this number by ten, move the figures *one column to the right:*

0 · 0 0 1

The result is **one thousandth** ($\frac{1}{1000}$)

$\frac{1}{100} \div 10 = \frac{1}{1000}$

1 hundredth = 10 thousandths ($\frac{1}{100} = \frac{10}{1000}$)

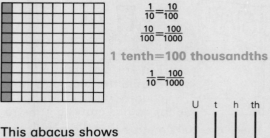

$\frac{1}{10} = \frac{10}{100}$

$\frac{10}{100} = \frac{100}{1000}$

1 tenth = 100 thousandths

$\frac{1}{10} = \frac{100}{1000}$

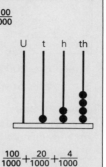

This abacus shows
1 tenth,
2 hundredths and
4 thousandths:

You can show this number in thousandths:

$\frac{100}{1000} + \frac{20}{1000} + \frac{4}{1000}$

$\frac{124}{1000}$ altogether

A Divide the number shown on each abacus by 10. Draw an abacus to show your answer:

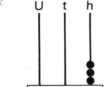

1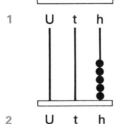

3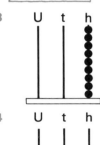

2
U t h

4
U t h

B Copy and complete:

☆ $\frac{4}{100} = \frac{*}{1000}$ $\frac{4}{100} = \frac{40}{1000}$

1 $\frac{1}{100} = \frac{*}{1000}$ 4 $\frac{7}{100} = \frac{*}{1000}$

2 $\frac{8}{100} = \frac{*}{1000}$ 5 $\frac{9}{100} = \frac{*}{1000}$

3 $\frac{3}{100} = \frac{*}{1000}$ 6 $\frac{10}{100} = \frac{*}{1000}$

C Write each of these abacus numbers in **thousandths**:

☆  $\frac{237}{1000}$

1 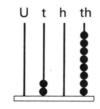   3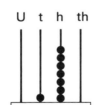

2 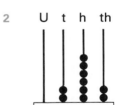   4
U t h th

D Draw abacus pictures to show these numbers:

☆ $\frac{138}{1000}$

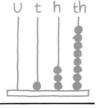

1 $\frac{164}{1000}$ 3 $\frac{321}{1000}$ 5 $\frac{107}{1000}$

2 $\frac{247}{1000}$ 4 $\frac{260}{1000}$ 6 $\frac{27}{1000}$

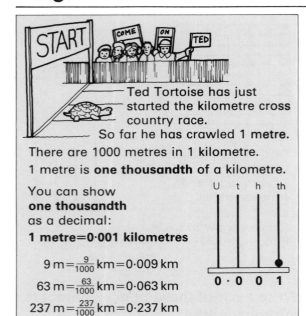

Ted Tortoise has just started the kilometre cross country race.
So far he has crawled 1 **metre**.
There are 1000 metres in 1 kilometre.
1 metre is **one thousandth** of a kilometre.

You can show
one thousandth
as a decimal:
1 metre=0·001 kilometres

$9 \text{ m} = \frac{9}{1000} \text{ km} = 0 \cdot 009 \text{ km}$

$63 \text{ m} = \frac{63}{1000} \text{ km} = 0 \cdot 063 \text{ km}$

$237 \text{ m} = \frac{237}{1000} \text{ km} = 0 \cdot 237 \text{ km}$

U	t	h	th

0 · 0 0 1

1000 millimetres=1 metre
$1 \text{ mm} = \frac{1}{1000} \text{ m}$
$1 \text{ mm} = 0 \cdot 001 \text{ m}$

The length of this line is 64 mm.
The length of the line, in metres, is
$\frac{64}{1000} \text{ m}$ or **0·064 m**.

A Write these distances as **kilometres**:

☆ 14 m *0·014 km*

1. 38 m
2. 74 m
3. 96 m
4. 132 m
5. 165 m
6. 283 m
7. 496 m
8. 528 m
9. 881 m
10. 999 m

B Write these fractions as **decimals**:

☆ $\frac{162}{1000}$ *0·162*

1. $\frac{336}{1000}$
2. $\frac{264}{1000}$
3. $\frac{408}{1000}$
4. $\frac{963}{1000}$
5. $\frac{713}{1000}$
6. $\frac{631}{1000}$
7. $\frac{78}{1000}$
8. $\frac{6}{1000}$
9. $\frac{91}{1000}$

C Measure the **lengths** of these lines as accurately as you can.
Write the length of each line in metres, **as a decimal**:

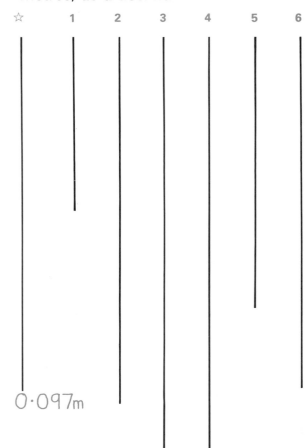

☆ 1 2 3 4 5 6

0·097m

Length

Master Blunder has written the lengths of these objects in metres:

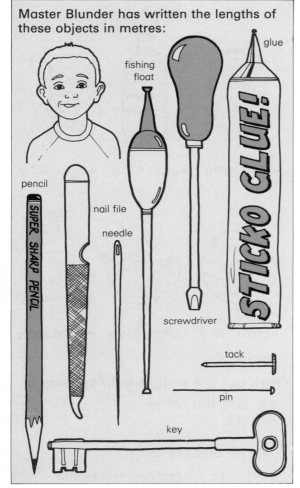

A Copy and complete the table below by writing the name of each object beside its correct length:

	length	object
☆	0·082 m	glue
1	0·077 m	
2	0·020 m	
3	0·070 m	
4	0·084 m	
5	0·063 m	
6	0·051 m	
7	0·075 m	
8	0·027 m	

Super Scientist has to lengthen some rods:

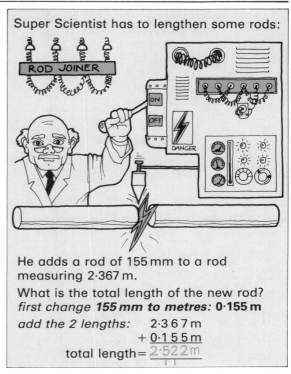

He adds a rod of 155 mm to a rod measuring 2·367 m.

What is the total length of the new rod?
first change **155 mm to metres: 0·155 m**

add the 2 lengths: 2·3 6 7 m
                      + 0·1 5 5 m
          total length = 2·522 m

B Work out the total lengths of these pairs of rods in **metres**:

                    0·086 m
                  + 1·382 m
☆ 86 mm and 1·382 m   1·468 m

1 1·329 m and 35 mm
2 65 mm and 1·886 m
3 2·932 m and 182 mm
4 429 mm and 3·772 m

5 1·068 m and 19 mm
6 6·851 m and 28 mm
7 2·496 m and 51 mm
8 826 mm and 1·309 m

C Write these lengths in **millimetres**:
☆ 0·531 m   531 mm

1 0·036 m
2 0·072 m
3 0·134 m
4 0·278 m
5 0·341 m

6 0·076 m
7 0·515 m
8 0·820 m
9 0·603 m
10 0·125 m

$$1000\,g = 1\,kg$$

$$1\,g = \tfrac{1}{1000}\,kg$$

$$1\,g = 0\cdot001\,kg$$

$$24\,g = \tfrac{24}{1000}\,kg = 0\cdot024\,kg$$

$$194\,g = \tfrac{194}{1000}\,kg = 0\cdot194\,kg$$

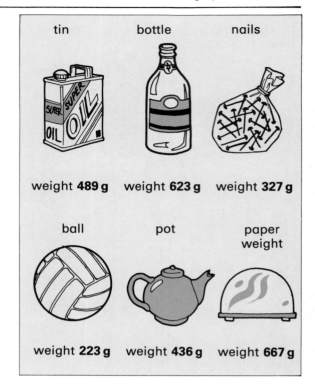

tin   bottle   nails

weight **489 g**   weight **623 g**   weight **327 g**

ball   pot   paper weight

weight **223 g**   weight **436 g**   weight **667 g**

A Write these weights in **kilograms**:

☆ 132 g   0·132 kg

1	25 g	6	307 g
2	76 g	7	385 g
3	185 g	8	409 g
4	109 g	9	637 g
5	137 g	10	845 g

B Write these weights in **grams**:

☆ 1·263 kg   1263 g

1	1·342 kg	6	2·371 kg
2	0·657 kg	7	0·604 kg
3	0·715 kg	8	1·361 kg
4	1·379 kg	9	2·222 kg
5	1·547 kg	10	3·159 kg

C Write < or > for ✳'s:

☆ 232 g ✳ 0·301 kg   <

1 463 g ✳ 0·376 kg

2 0·595 kg ✳ 512 g

3 0·355 kg ✳ 360 g

4 717 g ✳ 0·771 kg

5 600 g ✳ 0·598 kg

6 0·397 kg ✳ 395 g

7 627 g ✳ 0·606 kg

8 0·077 kg ✳ 86 g

D Work out the weight in **kilograms** of:

☆ the ball, the bottle and the pot

$$\begin{array}{r} 223\,g \\ 623\,g \\ +436\,g \\ \hline 1282\,g \end{array} \quad 1\cdot282\ kg$$

1 the ball and the tin   1282 g   1·282 kg

2 the paper weight and the bottle

3 the bottle and the pot

4 the tin, the ball and the nails

5 the bottle, the pot and the ball

6 the nails, the pot and the tin

7 3 pots

8 4 tins

9 2 paper weights and a bottle

10 2 bags of nails and a pot

11 2 bottles

12 3 paper weights

13 2 balls and 2 bags of nails

14 2 pots and 2 tins

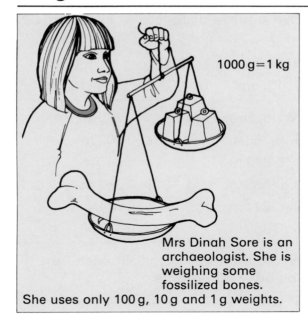

1000 g = 1 kg

Mrs Dinah Sore is an archaeologist. She is weighing some fossilized bones. She uses only 100 g, 10 g and 1 g weights.

A Copy and complete the table below. Show the number of each weight Mrs Dinah Sore will use to weigh each bone:

	100 g	10 g	1 g
☆ 628 g	6	2	8
1 847 g			
2 306 g			
3 762 g			
4 668 g			
5 950 g			

B Mrs Sore wants to record all of the bone weights in **kilograms**. Copy and complete this table:

	weight in grams	weight in kilograms
☆	628 g	0·628 kg
1	847 g	
2	306 g	
3	762 g	
4	668 g	
5	950 g	

C Write the total weight in each box below in **kilograms**:

☆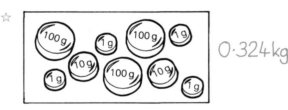

0·324 kg

1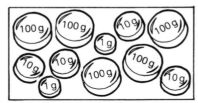

2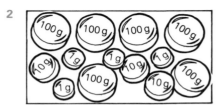

3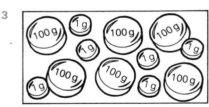

4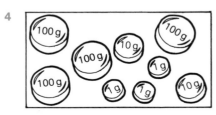

5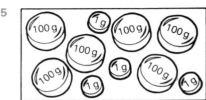

6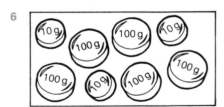

A How many **millimetres** in:

1 4 cm?   6 12 cm?

2 6 cm?   7 15 cm?

3 9 cm?   8 20 cm?

4 1½ cm?   9 25 cm?

5 3½ cm?   10 10½ cm

B Measure these lines as accurately as you can. Give each answer in **centimetres** and **millimetres**:

1 —————————————

2 ———————————————

3 ————

4 ——————————

5 —————————

6 —————————————

7 ———————————————————

8 ———

C Write these lengths **to the nearest centimetre**:

1 2·3 cm   6 17·4 cm

2 8·7 cm   7 6·5 cm

3 9·4 cm   8 9·5 cm

4 3·6 cm   9 18·5 cm

5 16·1 cm   10 20·5 cm

D Copy and complete:

1 $\frac{2}{100} = \frac{*}{1000}$ 4 $\frac{1}{10} = \frac{*}{1000}$

2 $\frac{8}{100} = \frac{*}{1000}$ 5 $\frac{3}{10} = \frac{*}{1000}$

3 $\frac{6}{100} = \frac{*}{1000}$ 6 $\frac{5}{10} = \frac{*}{1000}$

E Write these distances in **kilometres**:

1 26 m   4 237 m   7 100 m

2 84 m   5 350 m   8 600 m

3 136 m   6 850 m   9 400 m

F Write these lengths in **millimetres**:

1 0·263 m   6 0·602 m

2 0·512 m   7 0·340 m

3 0·638 m   8 0·262 m

4 0·241 m   9 0·01 m

5 0·350 m   10 0·1 m

G Write the total weight in each box below in **kilograms**:

1
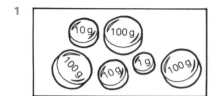

2
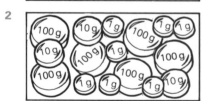

3
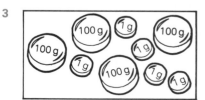

4
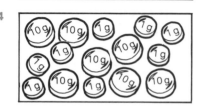

5
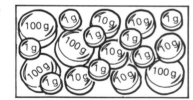

A This space snail moves at a snails pace.

It has a snailometer on its back to record how many centimetres it travels. The blue figure shows tenths of a centimetre or millimetres.

The snail in the picture has travelled 19·3 cm.

If this snail travels from the black dot to the blue dot below, what distance will then show on the snailometer?

snailometer reading (cm)	journey	new snailometer reading (cm)
26·5	A to K	
34·9	B to F	
176·1	J to C	

On a sheet of squared paper, mark ten dots at points where 2 lines cross. Label the dots: **A B C D E F G H I J**

Copy and complete the table by adding 7 extra snail trips of your own.

B Copy this number line:

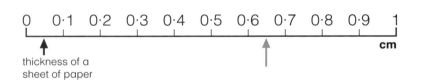

0   0·1   0·2   0·3   0·4   0·5   0·6   0·7   0·8   0·9   1

cm

thickness of a sheet of paper

The thickness of a sheet of paper is less than 1 mm so an arrow has been drawn to the correct section of the number line.

Find measurements in the classroom for each of the other sections on the line.

Example: a measurement between 6 mm and 7 mm would be needed for the blue arrow.

C Your school has been asked to store some TOP SECRET equipment.

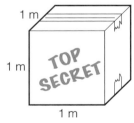

1 m

TOP SECRET

1 m

1 m

The equipment is packed in cube shaped boxes with each side measuring 1 metre.

It has been decided that as many of the boxes as possible should be stored in your classroom when it is empty.

Work out how many boxes you can pack into your classroom.

Answer any questions you can. Leave those you cannot do.

1 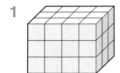 This cuboid has been made with centimetre cubes. What is its volume?

What is the volume of each of these cuboids?

2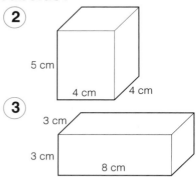

5 cm
4 cm 4 cm

3

3 cm
3 cm
8 cm

What is the capacity of this box in millilitres?

4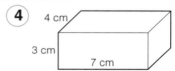

4 cm
3 cm
7 cm

Write these fractions as decimals:

5 $\frac{67}{100}$

6 $\frac{7}{10}$

Write these decimals as fractions:

7 0·3

8 0·37

9 0·07

Copy and complete:

10 3 6 · 8 5
   + 1 2 · 9 4

11 2 1 · 6 4
   + 1 4 · 9 5

12 2 1 · 6 3 5
    + 1 9 · 8 4 9

13 3 · 6 5
   ×   4

14 6) 23·94

Write these fractions as decimals:

15 $\frac{249}{1000}$

16 $\frac{403}{1000}$

Write these lengths in millimetres:

17 0·245 metres

18 0·806 metres

19 0·112 metres

Write these distances in kilometres:

20 318 m

21 279 m

22 42 m

Write these weights in grams:

23 0·328 kg

24 2·604 kg

25 5·101 kg

Write these weights in kilograms:

26 263 g

27 104 g

28 620 g

Write these lengths to the nearest centimetre:

29 8·6 cm

30 2·4 cm

31 11·5 cm

Copy and complete:

32 $\frac{7}{10} = \frac{*}{100}$

33 $\frac{18}{100} = \frac{*}{1000}$

34 $\frac{9}{10} = \frac{*}{1000}$

box 1
23 matches

box 2
33 matches

box 3
32 matches

If all the matches were shared equally among the boxes, how many matches would be in each box?

28 + 33 + 32 = 93

There are 93 matches altogether.

There are 3 boxes.

$3\overline{)93}$ ³¹

There would be 31 matches in each box.

The average number of matches in each box is 31.

This sort of average is called the mean.

5 pieces of string measure 26 cm, 38 cm, 41cm, 29 cm and 56 cm.

What is the
mean length of
the 5 pieces?

26 cm
38 cm
41 cm
29 cm
+ 56 cm
190 cm

$5\overline{)190}$ 38

The mean length is 38 cm.

A What is the **mean number** of:

☆ children in these classes?

class	number of children
1	32
2	25
3	30
4	21

$4\overline{)108}$ 27

1 coins in these piles?

2 marbles in these bags?

3 spots on these snakes?

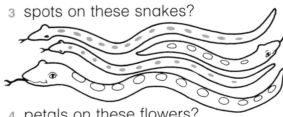

4 petals on these flowers?

B Work out:

☆ the mean weight of these children:

24 kg   37kg   29kg   42kg

132 kg ÷ 4 = 33 kg

mean weight 33 kg

1 the mean capacity of these 3 dishes:

846 ml   569 ml   640 ml

2 the mean time taken to run 200 m for these 4 athletes:

Bill
28
seconds

Tom
26
seconds

Long
John
89
seconds

Superman
1 second

3 the mean volume of these 5 blocks:

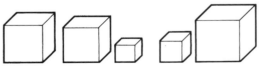

32 cm² 30 cm² 14 cm² 18 cm² 36 cm²

4 the mean area of these 4 lawns:

6 m / 6 m   14 m / 5 m   3 m / 6 m   4 m / 6 m

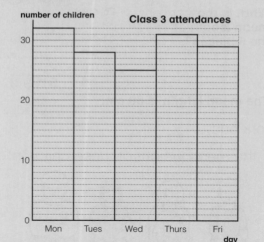

This graph shows one week's attendances for Class 3:

Class 3 attendances

The lowest attendance is 25, the highest attendance is 32.
The range of attendances is 32–25
The range of attendances is 7

A What was the total number of attendances on:

☆ Monday? *32*

1 Tuesday?   3 Thursday?

2 Wednesday?   4 Friday?

B 1 On how many days did the children come to school?

2 What was the mean daily attendance?

3 On which days was the attendance higher than the mean attendance?

4 On which days was the attendance lower than the mean attendance?

C Work out the **mean** daily attendance and the range of attendances for these classes:

	Mon	Tues	Wed	Thurs	Fri	
Class 1	26	21	20	24	19	*class 1*
Class 2	29	25	26	24	26	*mean*
Class 3	19	23	23	21	24	*22*
Class 4	31	32	28	27	27	*range 7*

D This graph shows the cost of 6 toys. Give the **range** of costs and work out the **mean cost** of the toys.

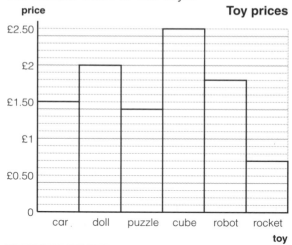

Toy prices

E This graph shows the marks of 7 children in a spelling test. Give the **range** of marks and work out the **mean mark**.

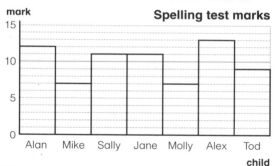

Spelling test marks

F This graph shows the spans of 5 children. Give the **range** of spans and work out the **mean span**.

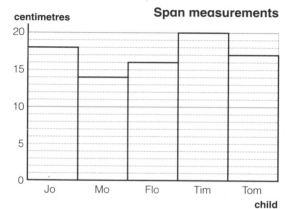

Span measurements

Averages

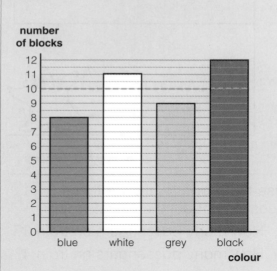

This graph shows the blocks in 4 building sets:

number of blocks

colour

The blue dotted line shows the mean number of blocks in the sets.

You can see that the mean is a number between the smallest number and the largest number.

A Use the graph to answer these questions:

☆ How many blocks are there in the blue building set?   8

1 How many different building sets are there?

2 How many blocks altogether in the 4 sets?

3 What is the range of numbers of blocks in the 4 sets?

4 Which sets have more than the mean number?

5 Which sets have less than the mean number?

6 On the graph, how many blocks are there above the mean line

7 How many blocks are needed to build up the blue and grey columns to the mean line?

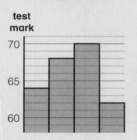

This is the top part of a graph showing 4 children's marks in a test:

test mark

From the graph you can tell that the mean mark will be between 62 and 70.

$$4\overline{)26^24}$$

The mean mark is 66

B The top parts of the graphs below show the test marks for 4 children. First **estimate**, and then **work out**, the **mean mark** for each test:

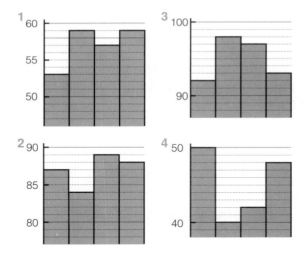

C First **estimate** and then **work out** the **mean price** in each group below:

1 36p   42p   45p   41p   41p

2 25p   33p   47p   46p   44p   45p

3 £16   £18   £15   £19

4 85p   79p   87p   82p   92p

5 93p   97p   £1.28   £1.30

6 £2.26   £2.04   £1.97   £2.13

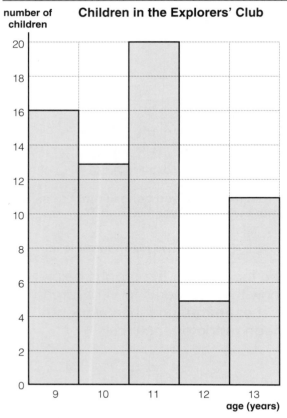

number of children

Children in the Explorers' Club

age (years)

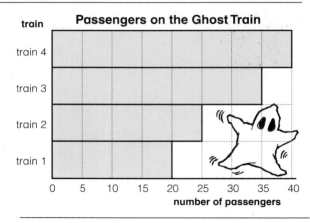

train

Passengers on the Ghost Train

number of passengers

A Use the column graph to answer these questions about the Explorers' Club:

☆ How many children are over eleven years old?　16

1 How many children are under eleven years old?

2 How many children are over ten years old?

3 How many more 9 year old children than 12 year old children are there?

4 How many children altogether are 10, 11 or 12 years old?

5 Are there more children under 10 than there are over 11?

6 How many children altogether belong to the Explorers' Club?

7 $\frac{1}{5}$ of the children go to camp. How many children is this?

B Use the graph to answer these questions about the Ghost Train:

☆ How many passengers on train 3?　35

1 How many passengers on train 4?

2 How many more passengers on train 4 than on train 1?

3 How many passengers altogether on the four trains?

4 What is the mean number of passengers on the four trains?

C This table shows maximum temperatures during the first week in May:

date in May	1st	2nd	3rd	4th	5th	6th	7th
max temp	14°C	11°C	9°C	12°C	8°C	10°C	13°C

Use the table to copy and complete this vertical graph:

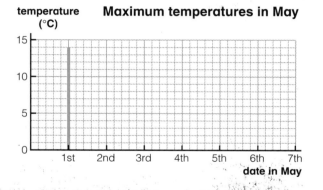

temperature (°C)

Maximum temperatures in May

date in May

Graphs

This table shows the cost of potatoes:

weight in kilograms	1	2	3	4	5	6
cost	20p	40p	60p	80p	£1	£1·20

You can show these costs on a graph by marking crosses:

Cost of potatoes

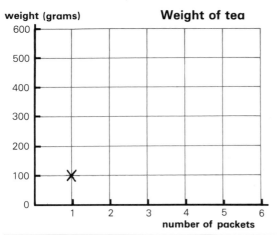

By joining the crosses with a straight line, you can draw a **straight line graph**.

A There are 100 grams of tea in a packet. Copy and complete this table:

number of packets	1	2	3	4	5	6
weight of tea	100g	200g				

B Copy and complete this **straight line graph**:

Weight of tea

weight (grams)

C This graph shows the cost of fruit crush:

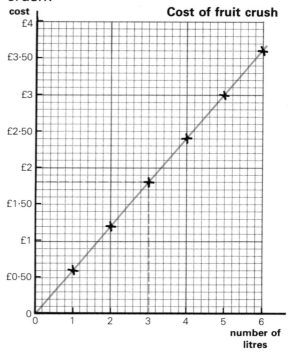

Cost of fruit crush

Use the straight line graph to answer these questions:

☆ What is the cost of 3 litres of fruit crush? *£1·80*

1 What is the cost of 2 litres of fruit crush?

2 What is the cost of 5 litres of fruit crush?

3 How much fruit crush can you buy for £2·40?

4 If you have £1, can you buy 2 litres of fruit crush?

5 How much change from £4 when you buy 6 litres of fruit crush?

6 How much change from £2·50 when you buy 4 litres of fruit crush?

7 How much fruit crush can you buy for £3·60?

8 How much change from £5 when you buy 2 litres of fruit crush?

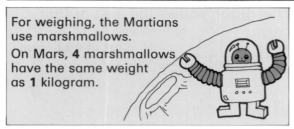

For weighing, the Martians use marshmallows.

On Mars, **4** marshmallows have the same weight as **1** kilogram.

A Copy and complete this table:

weight in kilograms	1	2	3	4	5	6
weight in marshmallows						

B Copy and complete this straight line graph:

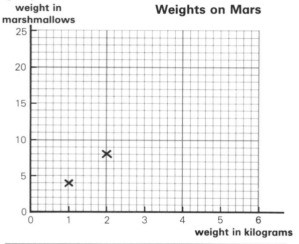

Weights on Mars

C Use your straight line graph to answer these questions:

☆ How many marshmallows have the same weight as 3 kilograms?   12

1 How many kilograms have the same weight as 20 marshmallows?

2 How many marshmallows have the same weight as 6 kilograms?

3 Give the weights of these items in kilograms:

mars bar **4 marshmallows**

mask **8 marshmallows**

flying cup **24 marshmallows**

martian marrow **12 marshmallows**

Each side of this regular hexagon is 1 cm long.

The perimeter is 6 cm.

D Copy and complete this table about regular hexagons:

length of each side	1 cm	2 cm	3 cm	4 cm
perimeter	6cm			

E Copy and complete this straight line graph:

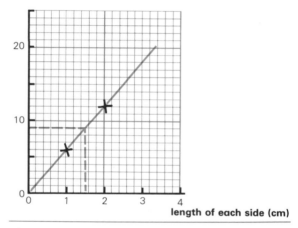

Perimeters of regular hexagons

F Use your straight line graph to answer these questions:

☆ What is the perimeter of a regular hexagon with a side of 1½ cm?   9 cm

1 What is the perimeter of a regular hexagon with a side of 2½ cm?

2 What is the perimeter of a regular hexagon with a side of 3½ cm?

3 If a regular hexagon has a perimeter of 24 cm, what is the length of each side?

4 If a regular hexagon has a perimeter of 3 cm, what is the length of each side?

5 Which covers more area, a regular hexagon of side 3 cm, or a hexagon with a perimeter of 24 cm?

Graphs

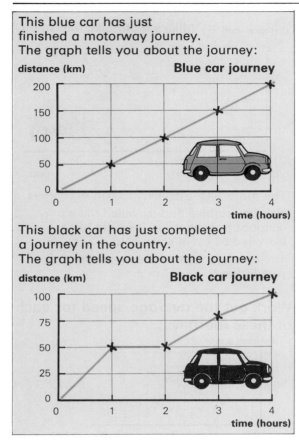

This blue car has just finished a motorway journey. The graph tells you about the journey:

Blue car journey

distance (km)

This black car has just completed a journey in the country. The graph tells you about the journey:

Black car journey

distance (km)

A Use the graphs to answer these questions:

☆ How far did the blue car travel altogether?   200km

1 How far did the black car travel altogether?

2 Copy and complete:

| time | distance travelled | |
	blue car	black car
1st hour		
2nd hour	50km	
3rd hour		30 km
4th hour		

3 In which hour did the driver of the black car stop for lunch?

4 Try to explain why the driver of the blue car was able to travel the same distance in each hour.

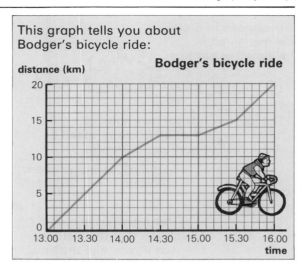

This graph tells you about Bodger's bicycle ride:

Bodger's bicycle ride

distance (km)

B Use the graph to answer these questions:

☆ At what time did the journey begin?   13.00

1 At what time did the journey end?

2 What was the total length of the journey?

3 How far had Bodger travelled at 13.30?

4 At what time did Bodger stop for a rest?

5 For how long did he rest?

6 At what time had Bodger completed exactly half of the journey?

7 How far had Bodger cycled at 15·30?

8 How far had Bodger still to cycle at 15.00?

9 At what time had Bodger completed exactly one quarter of the journey?

10 How far did Bodger cycle between 14.00 and 15.30?

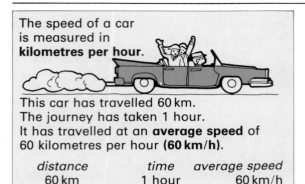

The speed of a car is measured in **kilometres per hour**.

This car has travelled 60 km.
The journey has taken 1 hour.
It has travelled at an **average speed** of 60 kilometres per hour (**60 km/h**).

distance	time	average speed
60 km	1 hour	60 km/h

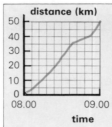

This graph of a journey shows that the distance was 50 km, and the time taken was 1 hour.
The **average speed** for the journey was **50 km/h**.

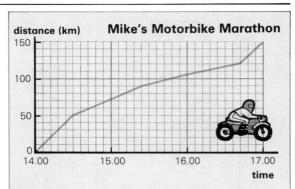

The motorbike travelled 150 km in 3 hours.

If the motorbike had travelled the same distance in each hour, it would have travelled 50 km in each hour.

The **average speed** for the journey was **50 km/h**.

A What is the **average speed** for each of these journeys?

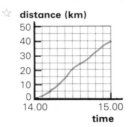

40 km/h

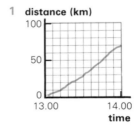

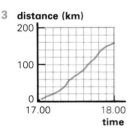

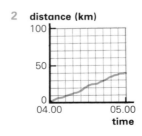

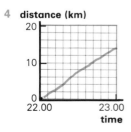

B Work out the **average speed** for each of these journeys:

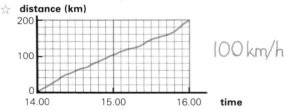

100 km/h

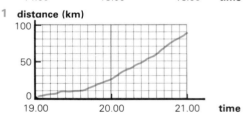

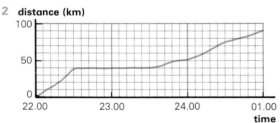

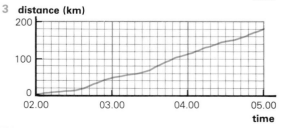

Graphs

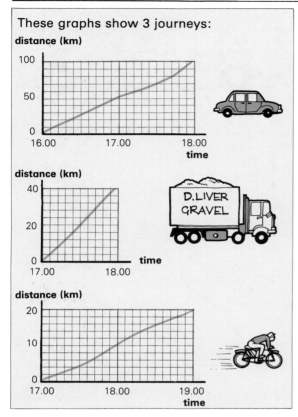

These graphs show 3 journeys:

A Answer these questions:

☆ What was the car's average speed?

         50 km/h

1 What was the lorry's average speed?

2 What was the bicycle's average speed?

3 Which journey was the longest distance?

4 Which journey took the shortest time?

5 How far had the car travelled after 1 hour?

6 The cyclist's average speed stays the same for four hours. How far does he travel in this time?

7 At the time when the car finished its journey, had the cyclist travelled more than 10 km or less than 10 km?

8 How far had the lorry travelled after half an hour?

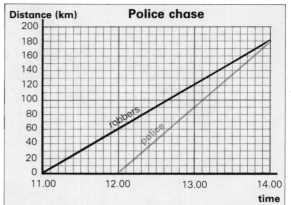

This graph shows that the robbers started their journey at 11.00, driving at 60 km/h.

The police started at 12.00, driving at 90 km/h.

The police caught the robbers at 14.00!

B Draw a graph to find out at what time the police caught these robbers:

☆

	starting time	speed
robbers	03.00	90 km/h
police	04.00	180 km/h

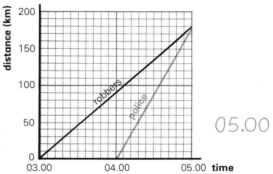

05.00

		starting time	speed
1	robbers	19.00	80 km/h
	police	20.00	120 km/h
2	robbers	16.00	75 km/h
	police	17.00	100 km/h
3	robbers	01.00	50 km/h
	police	01.30	60 km/h
4	robbers	04.30	70 km/h
	police	05.00	80 km/h

A What is the **mean number** of :

1 flowers in each bunch?

2 fish in each tank?

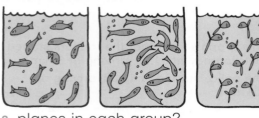

3 planes in each group?

4 draughts in each pile?

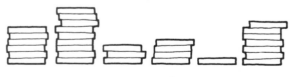

5 cakes on each plate?

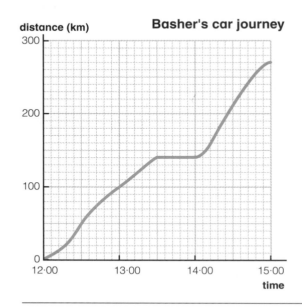

Basher's car journey

B Work out the **mean price** in each group:

1 84p; 81p; 89p; 86p; 85p
2 £62; £61; £63; £62
3 £40; £50; £45; £41
4 92p; 64p; 83p; 79p; 72p;
5 £56; £49; £55; £72
5 £15; £19; £26; £24; £19; £23

C Use the graph to answer these questions:

1 How far did Basher drive?
2 How long did the journey take?
3 How far had Basher driven after 1 hour?
4 How far had Basher driven after half an hour?
5 Basher stopped for half an hour's rest. At what time did he stop?
6 How far had Basher driven at 2.30 pm?
7 Did Basher drive further between 12.00 and 13.00 or between 14.00 and 15.00?
8 What was Basher's average speed during the first 2 hours?
9 What was Basher's average speed for the whole journey?

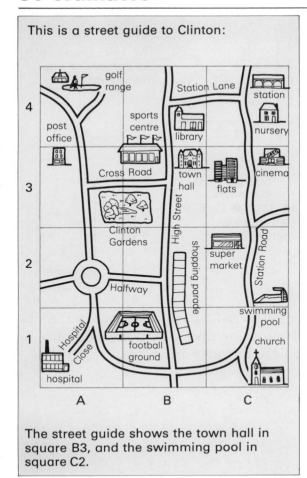

This is a street guide to Clinton:

The street guide shows the town hall in square B3, and the swimming pool in square C2.

Sometimes you need to fix positions accurately:

Devil's Island

You can show the position of different points on the island by using co-ordinates. The co-ordinates of the pine tree are (2, 5). (2, 5) means, start at the bottom left hand corner and count 2 lines across, then 5 lines up.

A In which square is:

☆ the hospital? A1

1 the library?
2 the nursery?
3 the post office?
4 the football ground?
5 the flats?

6 the sports centre?
7 the station?
8 the golf range?
9 the supermarket?
10 the roundabout?

B In which 2 squares is:

☆ Halfway? A2 and B2

1 Cross Road?
2 Station Lane?
3 Clinton Gardens?
4 the shopping parade?

C What would you find at these points?

☆ (4, 9)   Fearful Valley

1 (6, 8)
2 (3, 3)
3 (8, 6)
4 (1, 6)
5 (1, 1)
6 (7, 4)

D Write the **co-ordinates** of:

☆ Gull Island   (1, 10)

1 the tent
2 the food store
3 the hut
4 the rocks

5 the bonfire
6 the cave
7 the wood pile
8 the stockade

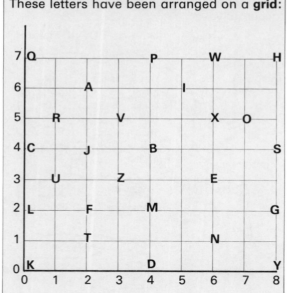

These letters have been arranged on a **grid**:

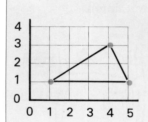

The co-ordinates of the corners of this triangle are: (1, 1) (4, 3) (5, 1)

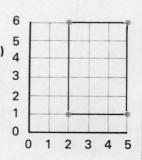

If you join these corners, **(2, 1) (2, 6) (5, 6) (5, 1)** you make a rectangle.

A Write the letter you find at each of these positions.
Each line makes a word:

☆ (8, 7) (7, 5) (6, 7)   HOW

1 (7, 5) (0, 2) (4, 0)

2 (2, 6) (1, 5) (6, 3)

3 (8, 0) (7, 5) (1, 3)

B Answer the question you found in **A** by using **co-ordinates**.
Start like this:

(5, 6)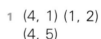
(2, 6) (4, 2)

C Use the grid to work out this question:

☆ (4, 0) (7, 5)   do

1 (8, 0) (7, 5) (1, 3)

2 (6, 3) (6, 1) (2, 4) (7, 5) (8, 0)

3 (4, 7) (7, 5) (4, 7)

4 (4, 2) (1, 3) (8, 4) (5, 6) (0, 4)

D Answer the question you found in **C** by using **co-ordinates**.

E Draw grids and join these sets of points to make **triangles**:

☆ (2, 1) (1, 4)
(4, 3)

1 (4, 1) (1, 2)
(4, 5)

2 (5, 2) (3, 0)
(2, 4)

3 (3, 4) (0, 3) (4, 0)   **4** (4, 2) (1, 1) (0, 2)

F Draw grids and join these sets of points to make **rectangles**:

☆ (0, 1) (0, 3)
(4, 3) (4, 1)

1 (0, 2) (0, 0)
(3, 0) (3, 2)

2 (1, 2) (1, 5)
(4, 5) (4, 2)

3 (0, 0) (5, 0) (5, 5) (0, 5)

4 (2, 2) (2, 3) (5, 3) (5, 2)

Co-ordinates

What shape is formed when these points are joined in order with straight lines?
(1, 1) (2, 4) (7, 4) (6, 1) (1, 1)

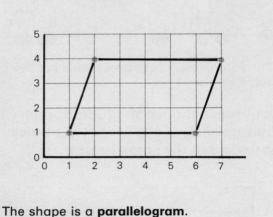

The shape is a **parallelogram**.

A Name the shapes that you find when you join these points in order with straight lines:

☆ (1, 1)
(3, 5)
(5, 1)
(1, 1)

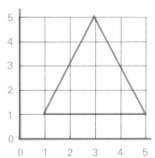

Isosceles triangle

1 (1, 1), (0, 2) (1, 3) (3, 3) (4, 2) (3, 1) (1, 1)

2 (1, 0) (1, 5) (4, 0) (1, 0)

3 (1, 0) (0, 3) (1, 4) (2, 3) (1, 0)

4 (0, 0) (2, 2) (4, 2) (6, 0) (0, 0)

5 (2, 2) (2, 5) (5, 5) (5, 2) (2, 2)

6 (2 1), (4, 5) (6, 2) (2, 1)

7 (0, 0) (2, 4) (6, 4) (4, 0) (0, 0)

8 (4, 4) (2, 2) (4, 0) (6, 2) (4, 4)

B Make 4 copies of this grid on squared paper:

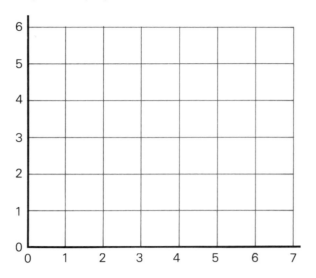

Form pictures on your grids by joining these sets of points in order with straight lines:

☆ (1, 0) (6, 0) (7, 1) (5, 1) (5, 2) (3, 2) (3, 1) (1, 1) (1, 0)

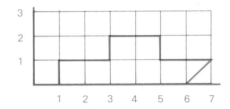

1 (1, 0) (1, 1) (2, 1) (2, 0) (6, 0) (6, 2) (2, 2) (2, 3) (1, 6) (0, 3) (0, 0) (2, 0)

2 (0, 4) (0, 2) (3, 2) (2, 0) (3, 0) (4, 2) (7, 2) (6, 3) (4, 3) (3, 4) (2, 4) (3, 3) (1, 3) (0, 4)

3 (0, 5) (1, 6) (2, 5) (2, 4) (5, 4) (6, 5) (7, 5) (5, 3) (5, 2) (4, 2) (5, 1) (5, 0) (4, 1) (3, 0) (2, 0) (3, 1) (3, 2) (1, 2) (1, 5) (0, 5)

4 (5, 1) (0, 1) (0, 5) (1, 5) (1, 4) (2, 4) (2, 5) (3, 5) (3, 4) (4, 4) (4, 5) (5, 5) (5, 4) (6, 4) (6, 5) (7, 5) (7, 1) (5, 1) (5, 2) (4, 3) (3, 3) (2, 2) (2, 1)

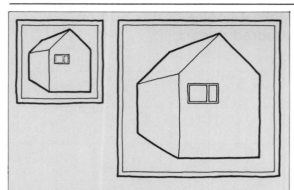

This photograph has been **enlarged**.

All the sides on the enlarged house are **twice** as long as the sides of the house in the first photograph.

The sides have **'increased in the same proportion'**

A Copy these shapes on squared paper and **enlarge** them so that the sides are **twice as long**:

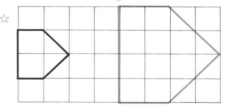

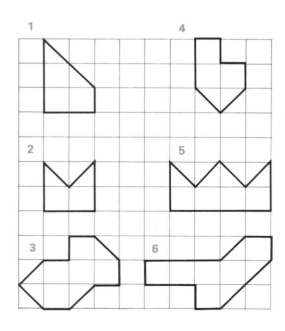

In this **enlargement**, the sides have **not** increased in the same proportion.

The enlargement is **twice as wide** but **the same height**.

B Copy these shapes on squared paper. **Enlarge** each shape so that it is **twice as wide**, but **the same height**:

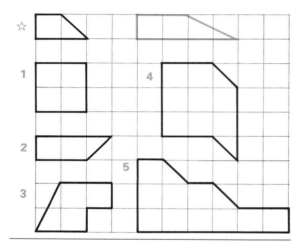

C Copy these shapes on squared paper. **Enlarge** each shape so that it is **3 times as high** but the **same width**:

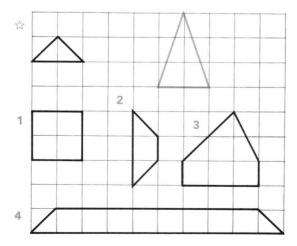

Enlargement

sides of shapes, areas 89

The **sides** of square **b** are **twice as long** as the sides of square **a**.

The **area** of square **b** is **4 times the area** of square **a**.

A 1 Copy this rectangle on squared paper.

2 Draw a second rectangle with sides twice as long.

3 How many times the area of the first rectangle is the area of the second rectangle?

B 1 Copy this square on squared paper.

2 Draw a second square with sides 3 times as long.

3 How many times the area of the first square is the area of the second square?

C 1 Copy this triangle on squared paper.

2 Draw a second triangle with sides 3 times as long.

3 How many times the area of the first triangle is the area of the second triangle?

D You need squared paper.

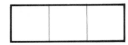

☆ Enlarge this shape so that the sides are twice as long.

1 By how many times has the area of the rectangle increased?

2 Enlarge this shape so that its sides are three times as long.

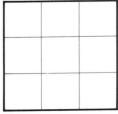

3 By how many times has the area of the square increased?

4 Enlarge this shape so that its sides are four times as long.

5 By how many times has the area of the triangle increased?

6 Enlarge this shape so that its sides are five times as long.

7 By how many times has the area of the parallelogram increased?

8 Enlarge this shape so that its sides are six times as long.

9 By how many times has the area of the triangle increased?

A You need centimetre squared paper.

1 Draw this shape on centimetre squared paper.

2 What is the area of the shape?

3 Draw a second shape with sides twice as long.

4 What is the area of the new shape?

5 How many times the area of the first shape is the area of the second shape?

B 1 On centimetre squared paper, draw a rectangle with an area of 12 cm².

2 Draw a second rectangle with sides three times as long.

3 What is the area of the second rectangle?

4 How many times the area of the first rectangle is the area of the second rectangle?

C 1 Draw a square with an area of 9 cm².

2 Draw a second square with sides twice as long.

3 What is the area of the second square?

4 How many times the area of the first square is the area of the second square?

D 1 On centimetre squared paper, draw a right angled triangle with an area of 4 cm².

2 Draw a second right angled triangle with sides four times as long.

3 What is the area of the second triangle?

4 How many times the area of the first triangle is the area of the second triangle?

E Copy these shapes on squared paper. **Enlarge** each shape so that the sides are **twice as long**:

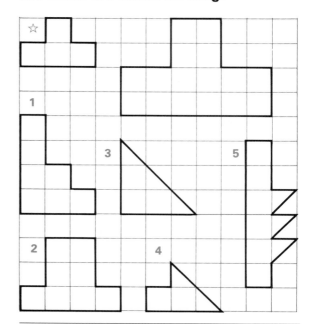

F 1 Draw Fred on squared paper.

2 Draw a new Super Robot with sides twice as long as Fred's.

3 What area does Fred cover?

4 What area does the Super Robot cover?

5 How many times the area of Fred is the area of the Super Robot?

Enlargement

On this grid, the sides of the letter 'N' have been enlarged to twice their length:

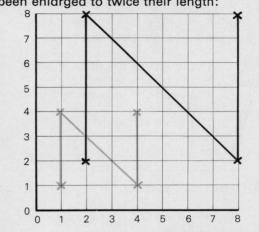

co-ordinates:

small 'N'	enlarged 'N'
(1, 1)	(2, 2)
(1, 4)	(2, 8)
(4, 1)	(8, 2)
(4, 4)	(8, 8)

To obtain the enlarged 'N', each co-ordinate of the small 'N' has been doubled.

A Copy this grid on squared paper:

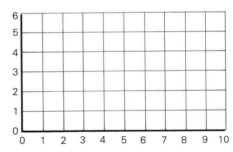

B On your grid, join these points in order with straight lines:
(1, 0) (1, 3) (3, 1) (5, 3) (5, 0)

C 1 Double each co-ordinate in **B** and write the co-ordinates of the five new points.

2 On the same grid, join these new points in order with straight lines.

3 Copy and complete: 'The new shape has sides ✱ as long as the first shape.'

D Copy this diagram on squared paper:

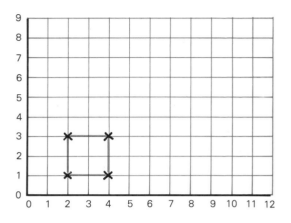

E 1 Write the co-ordinates for each corner of the square.

2 Multiply each co-ordinate by 3, and write the co-ordinates of the four new points.

3 On your grid, join these new points in order with straight lines.

4 Copy and complete: 'The enlarged square has sides ✱ times as long as the first square.'

F Write co-ordinates for the corners of:

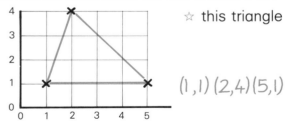

☆ this triangle

(1 ,1) (2,4) (5,1)

1 a triangle with sides twice as long as this triangle

2 a triangle with sides 3 times as long

3 a triangle with sides 4 times as long

4 a triangle with sides 5 times as long

5 a triangle with sides 6 times as long

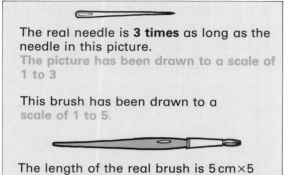

The real needle is **3 times** as long as the needle in this picture.
The picture has been drawn to a scale of 1 to 3

This brush has been drawn to a scale of 1 to 5.

The length of the real brush is 5 cm × 5 = **25 cm**

The length of the rubber in this picture is **1 cm**.
The length of the real rubber is **4 cm**.
The **scale** of the picture is **1 to 4**.

The length of the toothbrush in this picture is **3 cm**.
The length of the real toothbrush is **15 cm**.
The **scale** of the picture is 3 to 15 or 1 to 5.

A Work out the real length of each of these objects:

☆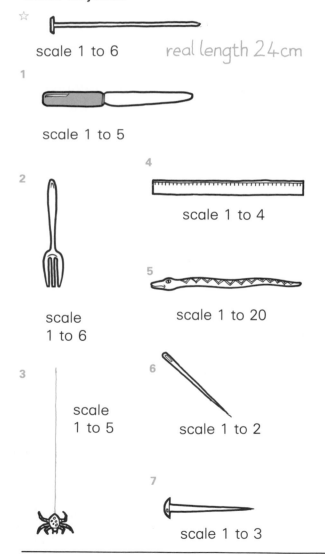

scale 1 to 6   *real length 24 cm*

1 scale 1 to 5

2 scale 1 to 6

4 scale 1 to 4

5 scale 1 to 20

3 scale 1 to 5

6 scale 1 to 2

7 scale 1 to 3

B Work out the **scale** of these pictures:

☆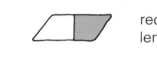

real rubber length 4 cm   *scale 1 to 2*

1

real pencil length 15 cm

2

real book width 16 cm

5 real spider's web length 30 cm

3

real circle radius 12 cm

4

real dart length 12 cm

6 real fish length 21 cm

Scale

Remember: 10 mm = 1 cm
100 cm = 1 m
1000 mm = 1 m

A This fish pond is drawn to a **scale of 1 to 100** or **1 cm to 1 m**:

☆ What is the real length of the pond?　　6 m

1 What is the real width of the pond?

2 What is the real perimeter of the pond?

B This garden is drawn to a **scale of 1 to 1000**, or **1 mm to 1 m**:

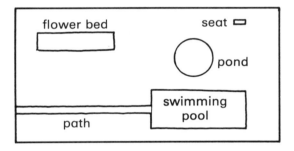

flower bed　　seat ▭

pond

swimming pool

path

As accurately as you can, work out the **real measurement** for:

☆ the length of the flower bed　20 m

1 the width of the flower bed

2 the length of the swimming pool

3 the length of the path

4 the width of the whole garden

5 the length of the seat

6 the length of the whole garden

7 the perimeter of the swimming pool

8 the shortest distance from the path to the flower bed

9 the diameter of the pond

This map is drawn to a **scale of 1 to 10 000**, or **1 mm to 10 m**:

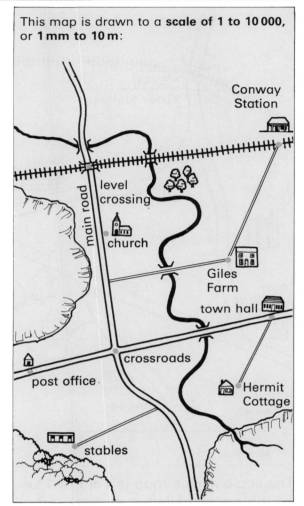

Conway Station

level crossing

main road

church

Giles Farm

town hall

crossroads

post office

Hermit Cottage

stables

C Work out these **distances** as accurately as you can:

☆ from Conway Station to the level crossing　500 m

1 from the church to the crossroads

2 from Giles Farm to the main road

3 from Hermit Cottage to the town hall

4 from the crossroads to the post office

5 from the stables to the main road

6 from the post office to the town hall

7 from Conway Station to Giles Farm

8 from the level crossing to the crossroads

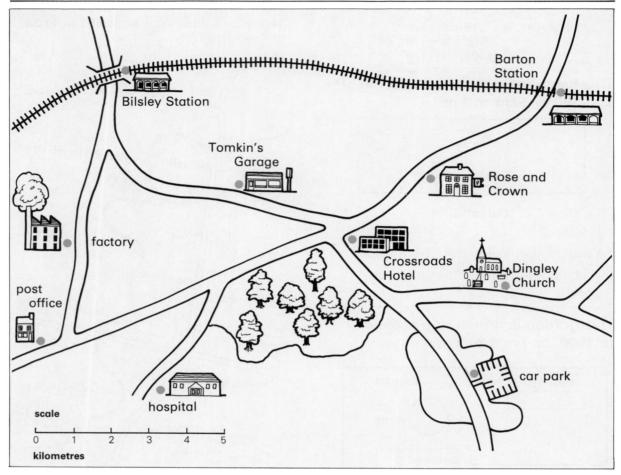

scale

0 1 2 3 4 5

kilometres

A The scale of this map is **1 cm to 1 km**. To the nearest kilometre, **work out the distance as the crow flies from:**

☆ Bilsley Station to Dingley Church   12 km

1 the post office to Bilsley Station

2 Barton Station to Tomkin's Garage

3 the factory to the car park

4 Crossroads Hotel to the factory

5 the hospital to the post office

6 the post office to the Rose and Crown

7 Dingley Church to Barton Station

8 the car park to Barton Station

9 Rose and Crown to Tomkin's Garage

10 the hospital to Dingley Church

B To find the distances below, lay a piece of thin string along the road, and then measure the string.

As accurately as you can, measure the shortest road journey from:

☆ the post office to the hospital   8 km

1 Dingley Church to Tomkin's Garage

2 Barton Station to the Crossroads Hotel

3 the factory to Bilsley Station

4 Tomkin's Garage to Barton Station

5 the car park to the post office

6 Bilsley Station to the hospital

7 the Rose and Crown to the factory

8 the post office to Tomkin's Garage

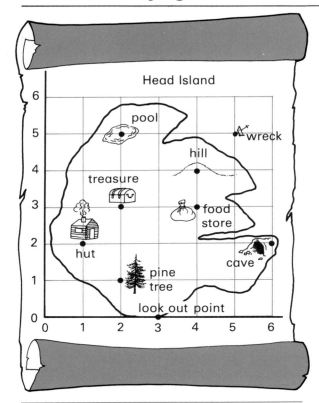

Head Island

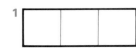

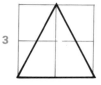

A Write what you find at each of these points:

1 (2, 5) 4 (2, 3) 7 (4, 4)

2 (3, 0) 5 (4, 3) 8 (5, 5)

3 (6, 2) 6 (1, 2) 9 (2, 1)

B Name the shapes that you find when you join these points in order with straight lines on a grid:

1 (1, 1) (2, 4) (3, 1) (1, 1)

2 (5, 6) (6, 4) (3, 4) (2, 6) (5, 6)

3 (7, 1) (3, 1) (3, 3) (7, 3) (7, 1)

4 (0, 3) (0, 5) (2, 6) (3, 4) (2, 2) (0, 3)

5 (4, 2) (3, 5) (4, 6) (5, 5) (4, 2)

6 (0, 0) (2, 2) (5, 2) (7, 0) (0, 0)

7 (0, 0) (0, 6) (6, 6) (6, 0) (0, 0)

C You need squared paper.

1 Enlarge this shape so that its sides are 3 times as long.

2 Enlarge this shape so that its sides are 4 times as long.

3 Enlarge this shape so that its sides are twice as long.

D This map is drawn to a **scale of 1 to 10 000**:

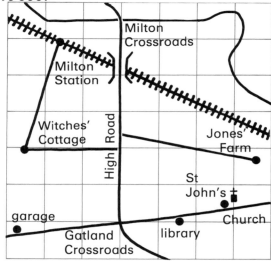

Work out the approximate distance of the journey:

1 from St John's Church to the library

2 from the Jones' Farm to High Road

3 from St John's Church to Gatland Crossroads

4 from Milton Crossroads to Gatland Crossroads

5 from Milton Station to Witches' Cottage

6 from Gatland Crossroads to the garage

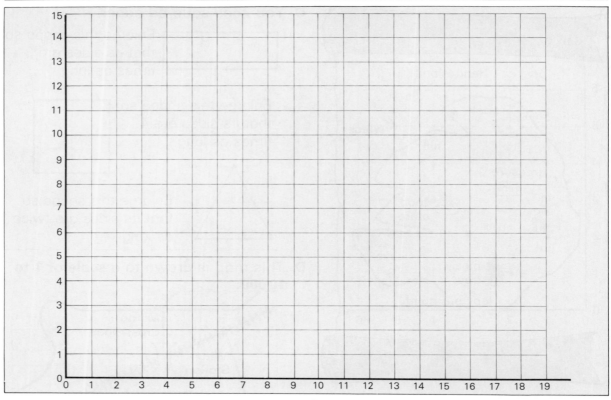

A Make 2 copies of the above grid.

B Join this set of points in order with
straight lines.
Do you find Windsor Castle or St
Paul's Cathedral?

(0, 6) (3, 6) (3, 4) (2, 4) (2, 6) (5, 6)
(5, 11) (2, 11) (2, 9) (3, 9) (3, 11) (0, 11)
(0, 0) (13, 0) (13, 4) (12, 5) (10, 6) (9, 6)
(7, 5) (6, 4) (6, 0) (5, 0) (5, 6) (5, 0) (14, 0)
(14, 6) (14, 0), (19, 0) (19, 6) (16, 6)
(16, 4) (17, 4) (17, 6) (14, 6) (14, 11)
(17, 11) (17, 9) (16, 9) (16, 11) (19, 11)
(19, 6) (19, 14) (18, 14) (18, 13) (17, 13)
(17, 14) (16, 14) (16, 13) (15, 13) (15, 14)
(14, 14) (14, 11) (13, 11) (13, 12) (12, 12)
(12, 11) (11, 11) (11, 12) (10, 12) (10, 11)
(9, 11) (9, 15) (11, 14) (11, 13) (9, 14)
(9, 12) (8, 12) (8, 11) (7, 11) (7, 12)
(6, 12) (6, 11) (5, 11) (5, 14) (4, 14)
(4, 13) (3, 13) (3, 14) (2, 14) (2, 13)
(1, 13) (1, 14) (0, 14) (0, 11)

C Join this set of points in order with
straight lines.

Do you find Notre Dame Cathedral or
Nelson's Column?

(7, 7) (10, 7) (11, 8) (11, 9) (10, 10)
(9, 10) (8, 9) (8, 8) (9, 7) (12, 7) (12, 15)
(17, 15) (17, 11) (16, 11) (16, 14) (15, 14)
(15, 11) (14, 11) (14, 14) (13, 14) (13, 11)
(7, 11) (7, 15) (2, 15) (2, 11) (3, 11)
(3, 14) (4, 14) (4, 11) (5, 11) (5, 14)
(6, 14) (6, 11) (7, 11) (7, 0) (0, 0) (0, 4)
(3, 6) (6, 4) (0, 4) (0, 6) (1, 7) (1, 10)
(2, 11) (2, 9) (4, 10) (6, 9) (6, 11) (6, 0)
(8, 0) (8, 3) (9, 5) (10, 5) (11, 3) (11, 0)
(19, 0) (19, 4) (16, 6) (13, 4) (19, 4)
(19, 6) (18, 7) (18, 10) (17, 11) (17, 9)
(15, 10) (13, 9) (13, 11) (13, 0) (12, 0)
(12, 7) (17, 7) (17, 11) (2, 11) (2, 7) (7, 7)

A You need a stop watch and 5 helpers.

Find how long it takes your partner to find the way to the centre of this maze and back again.

Record this time to the nearest second.

Repeat this investigation for 4 other children.

Work out the mean time taken by the 5 children to the nearest second.

Design a more complicated maze of your own.

Repeat the investigation with your new maze.

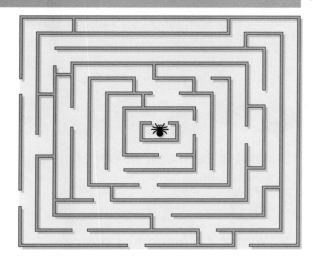

B

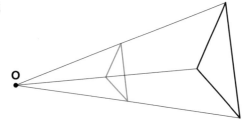

You can use this method to enlarge shapes.

Mark a point 'O' a convenient distance from the shape.

Draw lines from 'O' to the main points on the shape. Extend each line to double its length.

Join the ends of the lines to form the enlarged shape.

How has doubling the lines affected the size of the shape?

Use this method to enlarge a shape of your own so that the lengths of the sides on the new shape are twice as long.

Use this method to enlarge a simple drawing so that each side on the enlarged drawing is 3 times its original length.

C Work out a set of co-ordinates which when joined in order with straight lines will show a picture of your school.

You will find it helpful to first draw a picture of your school on a large sheet of squared paper.

After you have planned the outline of your school, you can add extra drawings to show the windows and any other features.

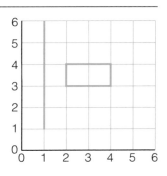

Example: (2,3) (2,4) (4,4) (4,3) (2,3) forms a window.

Answer any questions you can. Leave those you cannot do.

1 What is the mean number of spots on these ladybirds?

2 What is the mean weight of these gold coins?

 58 g 75 g 62 g

3 What is the mean test score for these 8 children?

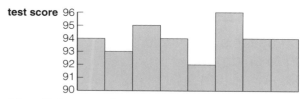

Use this graph to answer the questions below:

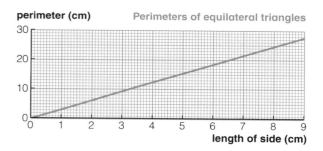

4 What is the perimeter of an equilateral triangle with sides of 6 cm?

5 What is the perimeter of an equilateral triangle with sides of 9 cm?

6 What is the perimeter of an equilateral triangle with sides of $4\frac{1}{2}$ cm?

7 If an equilateral triangle has a perimeter of $19\frac{1}{2}$ cm what is the length of each side?

8 If an equilateral triangle has a perimeter of $22\frac{1}{2}$ cm what is the length of each side?

Use this graph to answer the questions below:

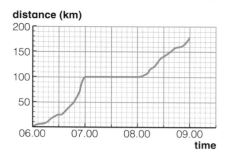

9 How far did Freddy travel altogether?

10 How far did Freddy travel between 06.30 and 08.30?

11 Freddy's car broke down at one point. For how long did he stop?

12 What was Freddy's mean speed for the rally?

13 At what time had Freddy completed half of the course?

14 The co-ordinates of 3 corners of a square are (2,0) (2,3) and (6,0). What are the co-ordinates of the fourth corner?

15 The area of this square is 9 cm². If the square is enlarged so that the sides are twice as long, what is the area of the new square?

3 cm
3 cm

Work out the real length of this creature:

16 Scale 1 to 7

What is the scale for this picture?

17 Real fish length is 32 cm.

Shape

Every day we use signs and symbols.

T means: You are approaching a road junction.

k + 3 = 16 means: when 3 is added to a certain number the answer is 16.

From this you can work out that **k = 13**.

A Work out the number that has been replaced by a letter in each of these questions:

☆ y + 7 = 15   y = 8

1 x + 9 = 26

2 m − 16 = 20

3 37 − s = 29

4 p × 9 = 72

5 56 ÷ q = 7

6 8 × t = 88

7 h ÷ 100 = 22

B In each question, the sum of the numbers in the square is the same as the sum of the numbers in the triangle. Work out the value of x.

 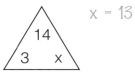   x = 13

1

2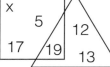

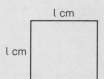

The length of each side of this square is l cm.

The perimeter of the square is P cm.

$$P = l + l + l + l \quad or \quad P = 4l$$

P = 4l is the formula for the perimeter of a square.

C Use the formula **P = 4l** to find the perimeter of a square with sides measuring:

☆ 6 cm   24 cm

1 9 cm

2 20 cm

3 $4\frac{1}{2}$ cm

4 15 cm

D Work out a formula that will help you find the perimeters of these shapes:

☆ **rectangle**   P = 2l + 2b

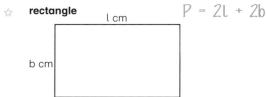

1 **regular hexagon**

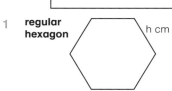

2 **kite**

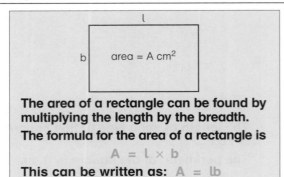

The area of a rectangle can be found by multiplying the length by the breadth.

The formula for the area of a rectangle is

$A = l \times b$

This can be written as: $A = lb$

A Use the formula to help you copy and complete this table for rectangles.

	length	breadth	area
☆	8 cm	9 cm	72 cm²
1	10 cm		80 cm²
2		5 cm	35 cm²
3	12 cm		96 cm²
4	16 cm	10 cm	
5		15 cm	1500 cm²

B The area of a parallelogram is **base** × **height**.

The formula for the area of a parallelogram is $A = bh$

Use this formula to help you copy and complete this table for parallelograms.

	base	height	area
☆	5 cm	6 cm	30 cm²
1	8 cm	4 cm	
2	9 cm	6 cm	
3	12 cm	7 cm	
4	50 cm	10 cm	
5	100 cm	35 cm	
6	9 cm		63 cm²
7	6 cm		72 cm²
8	11 cm		55 cm²
9	20 cm		240 cm²
10	100 cm		6300 cm²

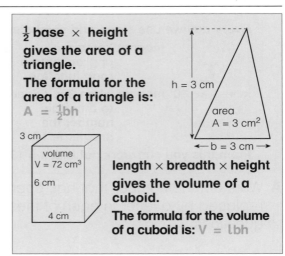

$\frac{1}{2}$ base × height gives the area of a triangle.

The formula for the area of a triangle is:

$A = \frac{1}{2}bh$

length × breadth × height gives the volume of a cuboid.

The formula for the volume of a cuboid is: $V = lbh$

C Use the formula $A = \frac{1}{2}bh$ to help you copy and complete this table for triangles:

	base	height	area
☆	8 cm	5 cm	20 cm²
1	7 cm	14 cm	
2	9 cm	11 cm	
3	12 cm	8 cm	
4	30 cm	20 cm	
5	13 cm	9 cm	
6	10 cm		50 cm²
7	8 cm		36 cm²
8	16 cm		64 cm²
9	20 cm		300 cm²
10	5 cm		30 cm²

D Copy and complete this table for cuboids:

	length	breadth	height	volume
☆	2 cm	4 cm	6 cm	48 cm³
1	3 cm	2 cm	5 cm	
2	4 cm	3 cm	6 cm	
3	2 cm	8 cm		64 cm³
4		5 cm	6 cm	120 cm³
5	5 cm		6 cm	300 cm³

Shape

This circle has a radius of 2 cm.

It has a diameter of 4 cm.

Here is a way to find the length of the circumference:

Mark a point on the circumference. Choose a starting point on your table. Roll the circle round until the mark reaches the table again.

Measure the distance the circle has travelled.

A Using the method above, work out the approximate circumference of a circle with a radius of:

☆ 1 cm *6 cm*

1 2 cm

2 3 cm

3 4 cm

4 5 cm

5 6 cm

B Copy and complete this graph using the information you have gathered.

Circumferences of circles

length of circumference (cm)

(graph with y-axis length of circumference (cm) from 0 to 40, x-axis length of diameter (cm) from 0 to 12)

length of diameter (cm)

C The circumference of a circle is a little more than 3 times its **diameter**. If any points on your graph do not show this, check the measurements for that circle again.

Here are 2 ways of measuring the circumference of a larger circle:

Place a paper band around the circular object. Make a hole with your pencil where the ends of the band overlap. Measure the distance between the 2 holes.

Lay a length of cotton or thin string around the circumference. Measure the length of string needed.

D Measure the circumferences of 3 larger circles using the methods above. Here are some ideas:

The top of a waste paper bin.

The wheel of a trundle wheel.

The top of a dustbin.

E Are the circumferences you measured in question D about 3 times the lengths of the diameters? If not, check the measurements again.

F Estimate the circumference of a circle with a diameter of:

1 12 cm

2 15 cm

3 20 cm

4 40 cm

5 1 m

Many years ago, the Greeks found that the circumference of a circle measures a little more than 3 times the diameter.

A Greek called Archimedes calculated that the circumference was about $3\frac{1}{7}$ times the diameter.

Now this measure has been calculated very accurately.

The value is called 'pi' and is written as... π

The approximate value of π is 3·14

The formula for the circumference of a circle (C) is C = πd. where 'd' is the diameter.

Often the formula is written as C = 2πr where r is the radius.

A Use the formula **C = 2πr** and a calculator to find the approximate circumferences of these circles:

6·28 cm

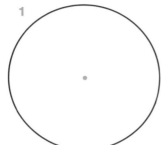

1

3

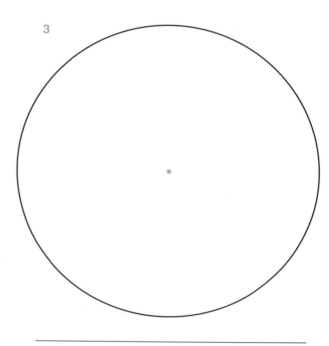

2

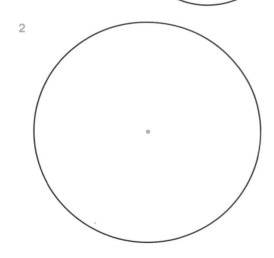

B Use the formula **C = 2πr** to find the approximate circumference of a circle with a radius of:

☆ 6 cm   37·68 cm

1 5 cm

2 8 cm

3 9 cm

4 12 cm

5 20 cm

6 1 m

Averages

Here are the shoe sizes for 9 children:

name	shoe size	name	shoe size
Alex	3	Balwinder	7
Anish	5	Alice	4
Jackie	6	Yoko	3
Micky	5	Billy	7
Joseph	4		

When these shoe sizes are put in order the middle number is 5. This middle number is called the median.

2 3 4 4 5 5 6 7 7

A Work out the range, mean and median for each of these sets of data:

☆ **name**	**number of pets**
Jack	1
Selina	3
Fred	4
Millie	2
Esther	2
Molly	2
Arthur	0

Range 4   Mean 2   Median 2

1 **name**	**age**
Adrian	8
Alison	12
Chloe	9
Doris	10
Kazué	11
Fred	10
Henry	10

2 **day**	**midday temperature**
Monday	17 °C
Tuesday	14 °C
Wednesday	13 °C
Thursday	21 °C
Friday	15 °C

Working out the median

drink	cost
Cola	52p
Fizz	46p
Squash	30p
Lemonade	35p
Juice	48p
Tea	48p

When these costs are put in order there are 2 costs in the middle...

30p 35p 46p 48p 48p 52p

The median cost is found by working out the mean of these 2 middle costs. The median cost is 47p.

B Work out the range, mean and median for each of these sets of data:

☆ **toy** | **cost** |
--- | --- | ---
doll | £1.25 |
puzzle | £2.60 | Range £1.72
ball | £1.47 | Mean £1.55
mask | £0.88 | Median £1.36

1 **name**	**height**
Zoe	1·60 m
Yvonne	1·63 m
Xavier	1·48 m
William	1·53 m
Veronica	1·70 m
Tania	1·66 m
Sania	1·46 m
Rohit	1·58 m

2 **athlete**	**time taken for race**
Sally	2 minutes 8 seconds
Florence	1 minute 58 seconds
Gemma	2 minutes 2 seconds
Anita	2 minutes 18 seconds
Mandy	2 minutes 23 seconds
Pauline	1 minute 53 seconds

Splutter's used cars – sales sheet						
month	Jan	Feb	Mar	Apr	May	Jun
cars sold	7	9	3	10	6	3
month	July	Aug	Sept	Oct	Nov	Dec
cars sold	9	22	16	4	3	4

In a set of data the number that appears most often is called the mode.

The number that appears most often on Splutters' sales sheet is 3.

The mode for the number of cars sold is 3.

Number of governors at school meetings

Month	number of governors
February	11
April	15
June	12
September	11
November	16

For this data the range is 5, the mean is 13, the median is 12 and the mode is 11.

A Using the data below, work out the mode for:

☆ the number of meals served:

day	meals served
Mon	82
Tues	80
Weds	86
Thurs	82
Fri	76

82

1 the number of drinks sold:

drink	number sold
lemonade	58
cola	72
orange	16
chocolate	14
tea	88
coffee	69
apple juice	14

2 the attendances of Class 6B:

December attendances for 6B			
date	attendance	date	attendance
2	32	10	28
3	31	11	31
4	32	14	31
7	30	15	30
8	28	16	29
9	29	17	27

B Work out the range, mean, median and mode, for these sets of data.

☆ SPOKE'S CYCLE SALES

Colour of bicycle	number sold
red	20
blue	2
black	12
white	12
green	4

Range 18
Mean 10
Median 12
Mode 12

1 Colours of cars sold at Boneshaker's Garage

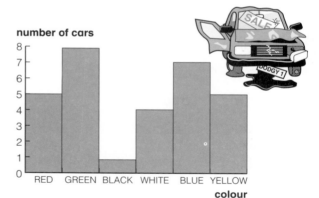

number of cars

| | RED | GREEN | BLACK | WHITE | BLUE | YELLOW |
colour

2 Meals sold at Sam's Cafe

Lasagne	48	Pizza	20
Fish pie	60	Roast beef	12
Burger	21	Salad	19
Sausages	16	Omelette	19
Soup	18	Spaghetti	27

Graphs

These are the scores of 2 players in a darts match.

Bulls-eye Bill
16 86 92 140 26 92 83 64 26 16
22 60 55 31 160 39 120 75 80 82

Hot-shot Harriet
52 62 80 26 33 28 100 140 35 48
69 50 15 88 63 49 100 14 66 97

You can show all these scores on a **frequency diagram**.

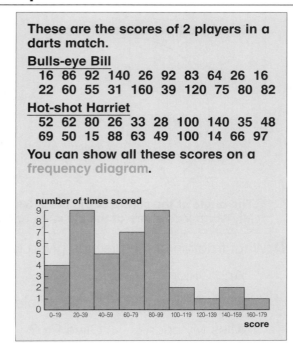

A On the **frequency diagram** above how many scores were:

☆ equal to 20 or more than 20 but less than 40?   9

1 equal to 80 or more than 80 but less than 100?

2 equal to 20 or more than 20 but less than 80?

3 equal to 100 or more than 100 but less than 180?

4 equal to 0 or more than 0 but less than 60?

5 equal to 40 or more than 40 but less than 120?

6 equal to 60 or more than 60 but less than 160?

7 equal to 40 or more than 40 but less than 100?

8 equal to 0 or more than 0 but less than 180?

Daily attendance at Stanwell School during June

346 374 348 365 348 357 372 368 360 361 353
351 345 342 339 335 350 357 368 362 360 371

From this information you can make a **frequency table**.

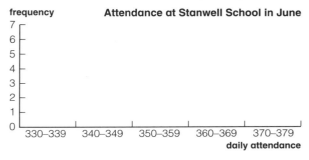

attendance	330–339	340–349	350–359	360–369	370–379
frequency	2	5	5	7	3

B Using the information in the frequency table above, copy and complete this **frequency diagram**.

C 1 Count the number of times each letter of the alphabet appears on one page of your reading book.

2 Now copy and complete this **frequency table:**

letter	A	B	C	D	E	F	G	H	I	J	K	L	M	N	O		
number on page																	

3 Copy and complete this **frequency diagram:**

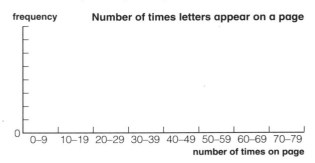

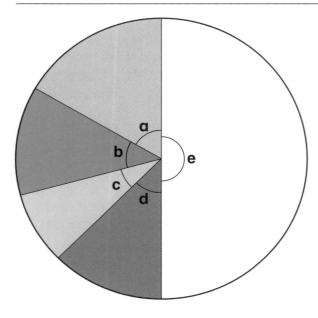

A Measure each of the angles at the centre of this circle. What is the size of:

☆ angle a?   60°

1 angle b?   3   angle d?

2 angle c?   4   angle e?

B What fraction of 360° is:

☆ 60°? $\frac{1}{6}$

1 30°?

2 180°?

3 45°?

C What fraction of the circle above is coloured:

☆ dark blue? $\frac{1}{8}$

1 light blue?

2 dark grey?

3 white?

4 light grey?

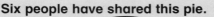

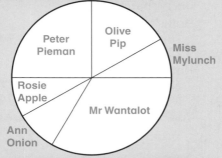

The angle at the centre of the pie is 360°
Mr. Wantalot's share of the pie is $\frac{120}{360}$ or $\frac{1}{3}$

D What fraction of the pie was given to:

☆ Ann Onion? $\frac{1}{12}$

1 Peter Pieman?   3 Rosie Apple?

2 Miss Mylunch?   4 Olive Pip?

E This umbrella has been divided into coloured sections

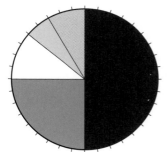

What is the angle at the centre of the umbrella in the section coloured:

☆ grey?   30°

1 dark blue?   3 black

2 light blue?   4 white?

F What fraction of the umbrella is coloured:

☆ dark blue? $\frac{1}{4}$

1 white?   3 light blue?

2 black?

This is a pie chart showing the favourite sports of 12 children.

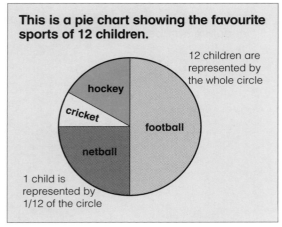

12 children are represented by the whole circle

1 child is represented by 1/12 of the circle

A What fraction of the children chose:

☆ football? $\frac{1}{2}$

1 netball?

2 hockey?

3 cricket?

B How many children chose:

☆ netball?   3

1 cricket?

2 football?

3 hockey?

C Draw your own pie chart to show how the people in the table below travel to work.

method of travel	number of people
car	3
bus	2
train	1
bicycle	2
walk	4

This pie chart shows how Ella spent her time between 5 pm and 6 pm.

1 hour is represented by an angle of 360° at the centre of the circle.

1 minute is represented by an angle of 360° ÷ 60 or 6°

5 minutes is represented by 6° × 5 or 30°

The angle at the centre for playing time is 90°. If each 6° represents 1 minute, Ella was playing for $\frac{90}{6}$ minutes. Ella was playing for 15 minutes.

D Between 5 p m and 6 p m for how long was Ella:

☆ talking to her mother   10 minutes

1 working on her homework?

2 reading?

3 eating?

E Draw a circle with radius 5cm. Divide the circle into 36 equal sections by measuring 10° angles at the centre.

On your circle draw a **pie chart** to show this information:

Favourite cars of children in class 6

favourite car	Ford	Porsche	Toyota	BMW
number of children	9	4	2	7

favourite car	Mercedes	Jaguar	Honda	Mazda	MG
number of children	3	5	2	1	3

In this diagram the blue horizontal line is called the x axis.

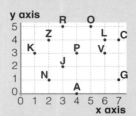

The blue vertical line is called the y axis.

When you fix a position you write the x co-ordinate first, followed by the y co-ordinate.

For the point P, the x co-ordinate is 4 and the y co-ordinate is 3. The position of point P can be written as (4, 3).

The x axis and the y axis can also show negative numbers.

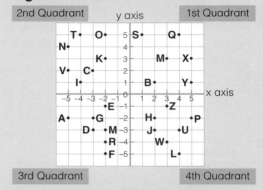

The axes form 4 sections. Each section is called a quadrant.

The co-ordinates of the point C are (–3,2).

The co-ordinates of the point R are (–2,–4).

A In the diagram above, what is the **x co-ordinate** of:

☆ the point **L**?　6

1 the point **A**?　　4 the point **R**?

2 the point **G**?　　5 the point **V**?

3 the point **C**?　　6 the point **K**?

B In the diagram above, what is the **y co-ordinate** of:

☆ the point **J**?　2

1 the point **R**?　　4 the point **A**?

2 the point **C**?　　5 the point **N**?

3 the point **V**?　　6 the point **G**?

C Which letters on the diagram have:

☆ an x co-ordinate of 3?　J and R

1 an x co-ordinate of 7?

2 an x co-ordinate of 4?

3 an x co-ordinate of 2?

4 a y co-ordinate of 4?

5 a y co-ordinate of 2?

6 a y co-ordinate of 5?

D Work out the question spelt out by these sets of co-ordinates:

☆ (2,–2) (–2,5) (3,–4)　　　　HOW

1 (3,3) (–5,–2) (–5,4) (5,1)

2 (–3,–3) (–5,–2) (5,1) (1,5)

3 (–4,1) (–5,4)

4 (–5,–2) (5,–2) (–2,–4) (–4,1) (4,–5)

E Answer the question in **D** by using co-ordinates to write a sentence.

Start like this:

☆ (–4,5) (2,–2) (–2,–1) (–2,–4) (–2,–1)
　　　　　　　　　　　　　　THERE

F In which quadrant is the point:

☆ (–1,3)　2nd quadrant

1 (4,–2)　　　　3 (–3,8)

2 (–3,–7)　　　4 (4,9)

Shape

These triangles have corresponding sides.

Corresponding sides have the same length.

AC = XZ   BC = ZY   and   AB = XY.

Each triangle also has corresponding angles.

angle a = angle x   angle b = angle y
   and   angle c = angle z

The first triangle would fit exactly over the second triangle.

When 2 shapes have corresponding sides and corresponding angles they are called congruent.

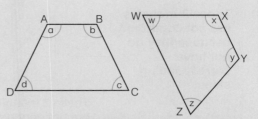

These two quadrilaterals are congruent.

They have corresponding sides:
   AB = XY; BC = YZ; CD = WZ;
          AD = WX

They have corresponding angles.

angle d = angle w, angle c = angle z
angle b = angle y, angle a = angle x

A Say if the following pairs of shapes are congruent or not congruent:

☆

not congruent

1

2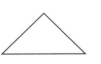

3

4

B Write the corresponding sides and the corresponding angles for these pairs of congruent shapes:

☆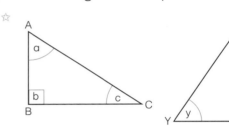

AB = YZ   BC = XZ   AC = XY
angle a = angle y, angle b = angle z,
angle c = angle x

1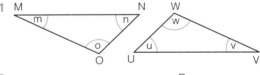

2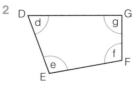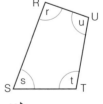

3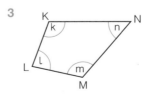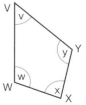

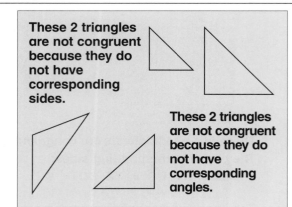

These 2 triangles are not congruent because they do not have corresponding sides.

These 2 triangles are not congruent because they do not have corresponding angles.

A In the diagram below there are 3 pairs of congruent triangles. Find the pairs and for each pair write which are the corresponding sides and which are the corresponding angles.

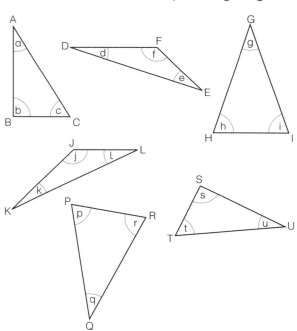

☆ Triangle ABC is congruent to triangle STU.

Corresponding sides:
AB = SU   BC = ST   AC = TU

Corresponding angles:
angle a = angle u
angle b = angle s
angle c = angle t

The diagonal on this rectangle forms 2 congruent triangles.
Triangle ABD is congruent to triangle BCD.

B For each diagram below, list all of the shapes you can find that are congruent to the blue shape.

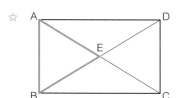

Triangle CDE
AB = DC   AE = DE   BE = CE

1
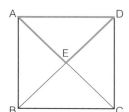

2
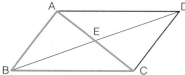

3
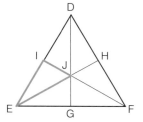

4

Shape

Place a mirror along the dotted line below.

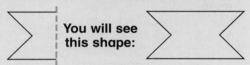

You will see this shape:

A On squared paper draw the shape you find when you place a mirror along each dotted line below.

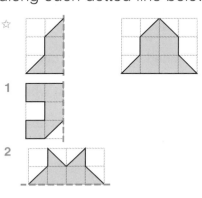

B Draw this shape with a dotted mirror line to show where the mirror must be placed to form each shape below.

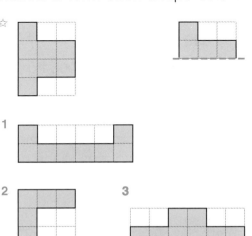

Place a mirror along line A so that you can see in the mirror 1 white, 1 blue and 2 black counters.

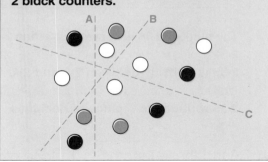

C Along which dotted line above can you place a mirror so that in the mirror you can see:

☆ 2 white, 1 blue and 1 black counters?   line B

1 2 blue, 2 white and 2 black counters?

2 3 blue, 3 white and 3 black counters?

3 2 black, 3 blue and 4 white counters?

D In each question below the second shape has been formed by placing a mirror on the first shape. Copy the first shape on squared paper and draw a dotted line to show where the mirror was placed.

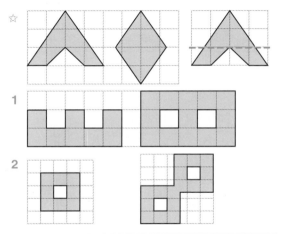

Here is part of a number line:

2·3 2·31 2·32 2·33 2·34 2·35 2·36 2·37 2·38 2·39 2·4

The number 2·34 is nearer to 2·3 than 2·4.

2·34 rounded to 1 place of decimals is 2·3.

2·35 is halfway between 2·3 and 2·4.

Halfway numbers are rounded upwards.

2·35 rounded to 1 place of decimals is 2·4.

A Round these lengths to 1 place of decimals:

☆ Worm. 8·75 cm   8·8 cm

1 Lizard. 14·39 cm

2 Slug. 5·21 cm

3 Centipede. 11·05 cm

4 Snake. 163·84 cm

5 Fish. 48·95 cm

B Round these numbers to 1 place of decimals:

☆ 149·82   149·8

1 36·28   4 316·66

2 34·25   5 18·04

3 111·11   6 16·95

Professor Precisely has measured this metal rod.

The length of the rod is 1·682 m

1·68 1·681 1·682 1·683 1·684 1·685 1·686 1·687 1·688 1·689 1·69

1·682 is nearer to 1·68 than 1·69.

1·682 rounded to 2 places of decimals is 1·68.

1·682 rounded to 1 place of decimals is 1·7.

1·682 rounded to the nearest whole number is 2.

Halfway numbers are rounded upwards. 1·685 rounded to 2 places of decimals is 1·69.

C Round these lengths to 2 places of decimals:

☆ 4·281m   4·28 m

1 2·893 m   4 3·555 m

2 28·625 m   5 26·449 m

3 56·656 m   6 11·985 m

D Round these weights to 1 place of decimals:

☆ 1·629 kg   1·6 kg

1 2·947 kg   4 1·006 kg

2 16·094 kg   5 9·899 kg

3 12·305 kg   6 15·955 kg

E Round these distances to the nearest whole number of kilometres:

☆ 3·649 km   4 km

1 46·243 km   3 34·099 km

2 12·556 km   4 92·255 km

Decimals

Joseph has divided 12 by 7 on his calculator. He does not need all of the figures that are showing.

To the nearest whole number his answer is 2.

To 1 place of decimals his answer is 1·7.

To 2 places of decimals his answer is 1·71.

To 3 places of decimals his answer is 1·714.

A You will need a calculator. Give answers to the **nearest whole number**.

☆ 36·32 × 3   109

1 25·94 + 17·63   3 12·97 × 3·9

2 516·52 − 49·013   4 45 ÷ 11

B You will need a calculator. Give answers to **1 place of decimals**.

☆ 62·3 ÷ 8   7·8

1 25·69 × 3   3 100 ÷ 3

2 57 ÷ 8   4 126·89 − 53·94

C You will need a calculator. Give answers to **2 places of decimals**.

☆ 80 ÷ 7   11·43

1 14·87 × 2·7   3 25·57 ÷ 11

2 29 ÷ 3   4 4·333 × 6

D You will need a calculator. Give answers to **3 places of decimals**.

☆ 19 ÷ 7   2·714

1 21·567 × 2·36   3 1583 ÷ 23

2 1997 ÷ 6   4 13 ÷ 6

When working with decimal numbers it is helpful to estimate the answer first.

8·83 × 4 = ✳

8·83 to the nearest whole number is 9.

9 × 4 = 36 and so you would expect the answer to be a little less than 36.

Using a calculator you will find that

8·83 × 4 = ⎡ 35.32 ⎤

E Copy and complete the table below.

In the 1st column write your estimate to the nearest whole number. In the 2nd column give an exact answer by using a calculator.

☆		estimate	exact answer
1	6·93 × 3	21	20·79
2	19·75 × 5		
3	101·19 × 7		
	990 × 98.63		
4	1100·72 × 3		
5	4·65 × 9		

F Without using a calculator, choose which answer is correct for each of these questions:

☆ 14·98 ÷ 7   2·14

  21·4   2·14   0·214   104·86

1 18·35 ÷ 5

  3·67   7·63   6·73   5·45

2 26·95 × 4

  10·78   107·8   1078   6·73

3 116·45 + 119·555

  23·605 2·365 2360·05 236·005

4 4·968 ÷ 9

  0·552   0·055   55·2   5·52

A 1 69 + 40 = ✱

2 Round 514 to the nearest 10

3 442 − 199 = ✱

4 Is 94° an acute, obtuse or reflex angle?

5 angle a = 100°
angle b = 45°
What is the size of angle c?

6 98 × 10 = ✱

7 570 ÷ ✱ = 57

8 $\frac{4}{5} = \frac{8}{✱}$

B 1 75 + 95 = ✱

2 £13·27 − £4·98 = ✱

3 Name this solid shape.

4 Three angles in a quadrilateral measure 65° 75° and 90°. What is the size of the fourth angle?

5 What are the factors of 28?

6 82 × 100 = ✱

7 Write the time that is 21 minutes earlier than 7.14 p m.

8 How much is $\frac{5}{6}$ of £36?

C 1 306 + 299 = ✱

2 Round 475 to the nearest 10.

3 What is the order of rotational symmetry for this shape?

4 What is the product of 9 and 12?

5 60 × 40 = ✱

6 8700 ÷ 100 = ✱

7 If a journey started at 6·42 p m and finished at 8·04 p m, how long did the journey take?

8 Write as a percentage $\frac{25}{100}$.

D 1 Round 6344 to the nearest 10

2 532 + 398 = ✱

3 Name this solid shape.

4 Is 236° an acute, obtuse or reflex angle?

5 917 × ✱ = 9170

6 9600 ÷ ✱ = 96

7 Write in figures the date: 15th November 1984

8 $4 = \frac{✱}{5}$

E 1 Round 7389 to the nearest 1000

2 £11·68 + £2·96 = ✱

3 Round 1850 to the nearest 100

4 What is the order of rotational symmetry for this shape?

5 In a right-angled triangle, one angle measures 38°. What are the sizes of the other 2 angles?

6 What is the mean age of 6 children whose ages are 9, 7, 12, 8, 5 and 7?

7 $\frac{5}{6} - \frac{1}{2} = ✱$

8 Write 45% as a fraction in its lowest terms.

F 1 Round £2352 to the nearest £100

2 What is the order of rotational symmetry for a regular hexagon?

3 Round £7500 to the nearest £1000

4 9 + 3 − 15 = ✱

5 48 × 20 = ✱

6 Is angle p acute, obtuse or reflex?

7 26 × 11 = ✱

8 Write $\frac{3}{10}$ as a percentage.

A 1 98 + 60 = ✳

   2 What are the factors of 32?

   3 Write as a decimal $\frac{4}{10}$

   4 $\frac{1}{3}$ + $\frac{1}{4}$ = ✳

   5 What is the time 22 minutes later than 12.22 p m?

   6 How much is $\frac{7}{8}$ of £64?

   7 What is the area of the blue triangle?

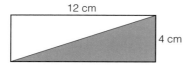

B 1 Round 629 to the nearest 10.

   2 Write as a fraction 0·6

   3 Write as a whole number $\frac{32}{4}$

   4 $\frac{7}{10}$ − $\frac{2}{5}$ = ✳

   5 Write as a percentage $\frac{9}{20}$

   6 What is the volume of this block?

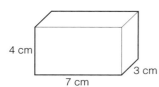

   7 $\frac{8}{100}$ = $\frac{✳}{1000}$

C 1 37 × 100 = ✳

   2 387 − 198 = ✳

   3 Rewrite this fraction in its lowest terms: $\frac{45}{60}$

   4 Is 181° an acute, obtuse or reflex angle?

   5 $6\frac{5}{9}$ − $3\frac{1}{3}$ = ✳

   6 What is the area of this floor?

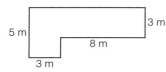

   7 Write in centimetres 183 mm.

D 1 Round 8800 to the nearest 1000

   2 77 × ✳ = 770

   3 How much is $\frac{3}{12}$ of £84?

   4 What percentage of this square is shaded?

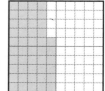

   5 How many millimetres in 11 centimetres?

   6 Write in centimetres and millimetres 22·6 cm

   7 Write as a decimal $\frac{273}{1000}$

E 1 3200 ÷ 100 = ✳

   2 Round the number 123·456 to 1 place of decimals.

   3 Write as a decimal $\frac{27}{100}$

   4 $\frac{3}{10}$ + $\frac{2}{5}$ = ✳

   5 A clock is $\frac{1}{4}$ of an hour fast. It shows 1.01 pm What is the correct time?

   6 What is the area of this parallelogram?

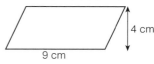

   7 What is the perimeter of a square with sides of $8\frac{1}{2}$ m?

F 1 What is the order of rotational symmetry for an equilateral triangle?

   2 £17.61 − £2.98 = ✳

   3 Write as a 24-hour clock time 10.10 pm

   4 Change this mixed number to an improper fraction: $7\frac{3}{5}$

   5 Give your answer to this question as a mixed number: $\frac{3}{5}$ + $\frac{7}{10}$ = ✳

   6 In a sale, a tea set costing £60 is reduced by 20%. What is the sale price of the tea set?

   7 What is the capacity of this box in millilitres?

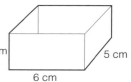

A 1 126 + 257 = ✱

2 $\frac{5}{6} = \frac{10}{✱}$

3 Write 8·7 cm to the nearest centimetre.

4 $2\frac{1}{5} + 3\frac{1}{2}$ = ✱

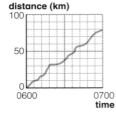
distance (km)

5 What is the average speed for this journey?

6 Write as a percentage $\frac{2}{5}$

7 It is 5 °C in London and −3 °C in Moscow. What is the difference in temperature between the 2 cities?

B 1 Round 1305 to the nearest 10

2 How much is 25% of £2?

3 Write $\frac{35}{60}$ as a fraction in its lowest terms.

4 How many millimetres is 0·128 metres?

5 What time is 37 minutes earlier than 6.18 p m?

6 Change this mixed number to an improper fraction: $8\frac{5}{6}$

7 6 + (19 × 2) = ✱

C 1 −6 + 2 − 3 = ✱

2 6250 ÷ ✱ = 625

3 Write 0·75 as a fraction in its lowest terms.

4 $4\frac{1}{3} + 3\frac{1}{4}$ = ✱

5 How many grams is 1·294 kg?

6 Write signs and brackets to make this answer correct.
9   5   7 = 44

7 What is the volume of a cuboid with sides of 5 cm, 6 cm and 10 cm?

D 1 57 × 100 = ✱

2 What are the factors of 48?

3 $3\frac{5}{6} - 2\frac{3}{4}$ = ✱

4 Write in kilograms 362 grams.

5 Write the co-ordinates for each corner of this rectangle:

6 What time is $\frac{1}{4}$ hour later than 22.52?

7 How much is 35% of £30?

E 1 20 + (20 × 100) = ✱

2 40 × 50 = ✱

3 Write 30·5 cm to the nearest centimetre.

4 In four tests Anish scored **23, 27, 19** and **27**. What was his mean score for the 4 tests?

5 Is 175° an acute, obtuse or reflex angle?

6 How much is 60% of £90?

7 Write the probability fraction for rolling an odd number on a dice numbered 1 to 6.

F 1 Which of these numbers is a prime number? **18 37 63 81 75**

2 7100 ÷ 100 = ✱

3 What is the perimeter of a rhombus with sides of 9 cm?

4 How many millimetres is 2·108 metres?

5 What is the mean of these 4 temperatures?

temperature (°C)
30°

20°

Midday temperatures

6 £2603 + £2997 = ✱

7 32 × 15 = ✱